Blackpool Tower

Front cover picture: *Blackpool Tower and the beach in the mid-seventies.*

Overleaf: *Blackpool Tower in the nineteen-sixties. The Palace was demolished in 1962 and the Central Station disappeared about the same time.*

Blackpool Tower

by

BILL CURTIS

TERENCE DALTON LIMITED
LAVENHAM . SUFFOLK
1988

Published by

TERENCE DALTON LIMITED

ISBN 0 86138 064 9 hardback
0 86138 068 1 limp covers

Text photoset in 10/11pt Times

Printed in Great Britain at
The Lavenham Press Limited, Lavenham, Suffolk

Contents

For
Peggy, John, Tania and Jo

Dedication

IN WRITING this history I have been repeatedly impressed and even awed by the sheer determination and tenacity of Sir John Bickerstaffe, who with great effort carried through an idea which on the surface appeared fanciful, ludicrous, even foolhardy. He was hampered from the outset by scheming financial manipulators and was beset for many years by a formidable shortage of money. He was, sadly, even reviled by his fellow townsmen.

Opposition faced him both in the town and out of it, but his dedication and faith in his beloved Tower never wavered. It is particularly fortunate that in this he was supported by his brother, his son, and particularly his nephew Douglas. Repeatedly Douglas refused to take holidays away from Blackpool, saying determinedly, "Who wants to go away from Blackpool and 't'Tower?"

It is with great pleasure, therefore, that one can add to this illustrious list of Tower owners the name of the President of the current owning company, Lord Delfont, who is—happily for us all—equally devoted to his Tower. The First Leisure Company, founded by Lord Delfont, has redecorated, maintained and restored the Tower both externally and internally, and continues to do so, high though the cost might be. As Sir John believed in anticipating his customers' changing needs, surely he would be very happy with the present innovations and updating.

I would like, therefore, to dedicate this book to the Bickerstaffe family and to Lord Delfont.

Bill Curtis,
Fleetwood, 1988

Opposite page: *The regimental band on the balcony at the front of the Tower awaits the arrival of King George V and Queen Mary during the Royal visit to Blackpool in 1913. The Tower has played a prominent part in local events ever since its opening in 1894.*

Acknowledgements

MY SINCERE THANKS go to the present and past members of the Tower management and staff for their co-operation and help, and their patience with my persistent questioning.

I am deeply indebted to John Thain for giving me access to his vast records and scrapbooks on the Tower and for sharing his extensive knowledge of the Wurlitzer organ with me. And I am grateful to the chief librarians and the staffs in the reference departments of Blackpool, Fleetwood, Wallasey and Morecambe libraries for going to a great deal of trouble to find relevant information and photographs.

My thanks also go to Mr Keith West, Mr Eric Redfern, Mrs Verren, Mr Harry Willacy, Miss Jill Chapman, Mr W. McGinty, Mr Charles Barlow, Mr Bernard Crabtree, Mr Peter Jay, Mr Norman Barrett, Mrs C. Cairoli, Snr, Mr C. Cairoli, Jnr, Mr Reg Campbell, Mr Brian Pengelly, Mrs Marie Winston, Mr B. Astin, Mr D. Sillcock, Mr P. Holley, Mrs M. Cregan, Mr Bernard Howard, Mr Alan Gaskill, Mr Albert Hamilton, Mrs Jill Steel, Miss Nora Gazey, Mr Rod Warbrick, Mr & Mrs Federman, Mrs M. Sutton and Mr Joe Hall.

Finally, my appreciation and admiration goes to Bob Malster, Terence Dalton's editor, who works tirelessly over my manuscripts to make them readable.

And also, of course, to my long-suffering husband, Colin, who patiently ferries me about on endless journeys, helps with research and technical details, and never complains (Well, hardly ever!).

Opposite page: *The Tower begins to rise above the Promenade in 1892 and already dwarfs the surrounding buildings. The base of the Tower is now hidden by the Tower buildings, for the Circus stands within the legs.*

Opening Day

1

"COME and see the tallest building in the country . . . higher than St Paul's Cathedral and the Great Pyramid" shouted the posters. And come they did. They came in their thousands on a cold windy Whit Monday in May, 1894.

They crowded the beaches, the promenade and the piers, and they simply stood and stared and marvelled. How could anything be so tall and slender? Would the wind blow it down? Some of them had never seen the sea or the sands in their lives before, but today these attractions paled beside the awesome sight of the Blackpool Tower, the tallest building in the country and the second tallest in the world. The tallest building in the world was the Eiffel Tower, opened only five years earlier in Paris, and the model for the Blackpool one; but as few people had any chance of seeing that, they were more than content to stand and view this magnificent structure on the Lancashire coast.

Mill workers from the grimy towns of east Lancashire and west Yorkshire, working-class folk who had scrimped and saved for this special day at Blackpool and the opening of the famous Blackpool "Eiffel Tower", which everyone had been talking about for months, they had arrived in more than five hundred special excursion trains.

Would it be as tall and impressive as the headlines had proclaimed? Yes, it certainly was.

On the journey, eagle-eyed trippers had vied with each other to see it first, a mere speck on the horizon; they watched it growing bigger and bigger, until they saw it almost unbelievably tall, towering gracefully up to the sky; seeing it from only a few yards away on the promenade, everyone was left speechless with awe. They searched for the legs to see what was holding it up, but the large handsome

four-storey red-brick building surrounding the base hid these from view. The building itself was impressive enough, with glass roofs, four turrets and two ornate pinnacles on either side, all leading the eye up the tapering latticework towards the flagstaff at the top.

They gasped as lifts filled with people soared up the centre of the tower; the lookout at the top was crowded with visitors who triumphantly waved to the saucer-eyed crowd below, craning their necks to look up. Who on earth could be so daring, so bold, as to ascend this tower, the earthbound people wondered. Three thousand were, apparently, for all day long there were queues of holidaymakers waiting inside the tower for the lifts to take them to the 380-foot-high lookout platform. The tower was 518 feet high to the flagpole and crow's nest, but an ascent to the glassed-in lookout point at 380 feet which held a surprising six hundred people (although the Tower's own advertisement claimed there was room for 1,000 promenaders!) was quite exciting enough. And if you wished you could walk up to an even higher platform, from where you could see for more than fifty miles into three counties, to the Welsh hills, to the Isle of Man, to the Lakeland hills, and you could trace nearly the whole of the Lancashire coastline. Oh, it was well worth the adventure of going up to the top; and all for only a shilling!

A ride to the top of the Tower in one of the two hydraulic lifts prompted a predictable spate of Lancashire wit: "I've never been so near to heaven before!"; "Ee, folk on't promenade look like fleas", and, to the liftman, "D'you ever 'ear 'arps up 'ere?", or "If I drop my clay pipe off't top can I get t't'bottom afore someone treads on it?" One exasperated liftman, having repeatedly heard all these and many more, said to his companion, "If one more person asks me 'Do I ever hear harps up here', I'll bloody strangle them!"

From the moment the doors were opened to the public on that Whit Monday morning 70,000 people queued to go inside the Tower buildings.

On the ground floor at the entrance was the

Opposite page: A circular stairway leading to the upper platform at the Tower top.

Left: John Bickerstaffe's Aquarium, modelled on the limestone caverns of Derbyshire, as it was at the beginning of this century.

Aquarium which, it was claimed, was the finest in the world. Some even said that it had been in existence before the Tower was built and that the Tower had actually been built around it. Entering the Aquarium was a strange and eerie experience; with its dim lighting the place seemed like some underground cave. As the Tower's programme said: "Walking along the quaint passages it would need little imagination to think one was walking along one of the Derbyshire limestone caverns on which the Aquarium is modelled. One walks among columns of massive rock, and long stalactites of all shapes and lengths droop from the roofs . . ."

Bedded in the rocks were large tanks containing strange-looking fish from all over the world, and at the end of the Aquarium was the "Grand Orchestrion", a large and ornate barrel organ which played continuously. "A very powerful and melodious instrument", proclaimed the programme; and for many years this was for many people their first introduction to classical music, the most popular piece being Tchaikovsky's famous *1812 Overture*, with *In a Monastery Garden* coming a close second. The Orchestrion was listened to by the hour by the entranced visitors.

For those who had never seen anything fiercer than the neighbour's dog or a runaway horse, a visit to the Menagerie was a fearful yet compelling experience. The smell was enough (to put it kindly, it was strong), but that just added to the exciting effect. Down the centre of the room was a three-step-high platform with a long velvet-covered seat; but no one sat on it, they wanted to stand as high as they could—and as far away as possible from the twenty or so cages lining the room and containing lions, tigers, monkeys, and even a fierce and noisy hyena, and you really kept away from him. Anxious parents watched in terror as their offspring made determined efforts to reach and stroke or tease the animals. Mum firmly gripped little Albert with his stick with the horse's-head handle to prevent him sticking it in the lions' cage.

Although many of the halls and lounges were still unfinished and not yet open to the

public, you could stay all day and listen to the day-long succession of concerts from 10 am to 10 pm given in the Pavilion jointly by the thirty-strong Tower Orchestra under the direction of Mr Oliver Gaggs (who had also composed the Water Ballet music for the circus) and the "Splendid Military Band" of the 2nd East Yorkshire Regiment, no doubt most handsomely attired in full dress to the delight of the Victorian ladies. And all this for a "nimble sixpence", as the advertisements said. There were even some stalls where souvenirs for Grandma and Aunt Bessie could be bought for a penny or twopence.

For another sixpence you could visit the circus, everyone's favourite; Queen Victoria herself had put her seal of approval on the circus, saying it was the ideal family entertainment, much better than the vulgar, bawdy music halls. There were three shows each day, at 11 am, 3 pm and 7.30 pm, and with an outstanding list of animal and acrobatic acts,

3

described modestly enough as "The greatest show in the World", the programme included Professor Nero and his four wonderful performing Indian Bulls. It ended with a spectacular water finale, the like of which had never been seen in a circus before; the building incorporated a unique sinking floor which could be flooded with nearly 40,000 gallons of water in one minute.

Taking part in the water spectacle were well-known swimming personalities, including the Johnson sisters, of whom Theresa was claimed to be the champion lady swimmer of the world. Apparently the whole Finney family were there in force, from Professor (there must have been no shortage of professors in Blackpool that year; there were seven of them in the circus!) Finney who was billed as the "Champion all round swimmer of the World", Miss Marie Finney, "Heroine of London Bridge", and baby Maud Finney who was head of the Water Fairies Ballet. Marie Finney's exploits at London Bridge were no doubt explained

fully to the admiring audience by the Circus manager, Mr George Harrop, who was also the manager of the Tower itself.

And if some were disappointed that there had been no official opening ceremony as there had been at the Winter Gardens sixteen years earlier, they were assured there would be one later when all the halls and lounges had been opened. Everyone agreed they would be coming back again and again to this unique building, and there were no real grumbles.

In the crowds few noticed the small, dapper man in his late forties walking among them, not marvelling at the sights but listening to the delighted exclamations of these first sightseers. He was well content with the views of the holidaymakers, but the predictions of some of his fellow townsmen that "It'll be a seven-day wonder" and "He's built himself a white elephant, I'm glad *my* money isn't in it" gave John Bickerstaffe room for thought. Were they right, after everything he'd been through? He sincerely hoped not; only time would tell.

The Emerging Resort   2

THE BICKERSTAFFE family had always been connected with the sea, being one of Blackpool's prominent fishing families; there had been Bickerstaffes in the crew of the first Blackpool lifeboat. As the resort grew in popularity, old John Bickerstaffe saw possibilities more rewarding than fishing and started to buy small plots of land as an investment for the future. His son Robert built the *Wellington Hotel* in 1871 on one of these central beach plots, and it immediately became a popular venue for visitors.

In the same year he bought an iron steamboat *The Wellington*, built at Preston, as a pleasure boat for the use of his customers, and eight years later he commissioned a paddle steamer which he called the *Bickerstaffe*, the first boat to run regularly between Blackpool and the Isle of Man. Later still he formed the Blackpool Passenger Steamboat Company, installing his younger son Tom as the manager.

Tom's older brother John, who had been born in 1848 in Hounds Hill, in addition to being a member of the lifeboat crew helped with the family businesses. He, brother Tom and cousin Robert brought new ideas and enthusiasm to the family's growing list of interests and ventures. A man of strong civic feeling, John became a town councillor in 1880, an alderman in 1887 and in 1889 was elected Mayor of Blackpool, an office he held for two years.

Like his grandfather and father before him, John began to invest in numerous ventures, buying up properties as and when they became available. He bought the South Pier hotel and shop from a Mr Marriott who, like many Blackpool businessmen, had suffered badly from one or two poor seasons. In course of time the Bickerstaffes owned much of the property on the promenade in central Blackpool, and later John was to buy a large plot of land behind the town which he sold to the local board to be converted into a park; it was named Stanley Park and later, ironically enough, contained a memorial to one of his greatest competitors, Dr William Henry Cocker.

In the early and mid-nineteenth century the railways brought visitors to the coast—staying visitors for whom the various seaside resorts in Lancashire were catering, wealthy middle-class people looking for cultural entertainment. On Sundays the working classes came for the day, but their visits were brief and as they had little

Left: *An early programme issued by Blackpool Pier, later known as the North Pier after the building of two other piers to the south. There was an Indian Pavilion at the pierhead for concerts and similar events, and also "commodious landing stages for the steamers to embark or land their passengers".*

Below: *The North Pier about 1880. The Tower would eventually occupy a site on the right-hand side of the picture.*

money to spend anyway, few efforts were made to cater for them. In the second half of the century, however, the working classes had more money in their pockets. They negotiated for annual holidays (without pay, of course) and thus they were able to afford a few days' or even a week's holiday. When they arrived at the seaside, however, the workers wanted more than soirées and concerts. Attractions which did spring up and blossom into popularity in addition to the music halls were song booths where all the popular songs of the day could be heard and sung to. Blackpool quickly decided to lose its up-market image and to cater for these new visitors, more so than Southport, Fleetwood or Morecambe, all of which fell by the wayside in the popularity stakes for many years.

The *Blackpool Gazette News* clearly disapproved of this trend, regretting the passing of the wealthy and upper middle classes in decidedly snooty tones: ". . . During the best months of the year the town is deluged by the lower classes, and it would be unreasonable to expect the higher grades of society to mix with them".

Blackpool's amusement caterers began to realize they had three priorities, to get visitors to the town, to take their money off them, and to keep them coming as long as possible; and they devoted all their energies and enterprise to these ends.

With few amusements to keep the visitors occupied, an iron pier built at the bottom of Talbot Road and extending well into the sea became an instant success. The Blackpool Pier, as it was initially called when it opened in May, 1863, enabled visitors not only to walk beside the sea but to walk on it in complete safety; nervous ladies were quietly reassured by the sight of lifeboats suspended at each side of the pier. It was very much an open-air attraction until its proprietors built a theatre called the "Indian Pavilion" at the end of the pier, adding tremendously to the pier's attraction. The Blackpool Pier (or North Pier as it eventually became known) also served another very important purpose in the town when the day trippers started to flood in: Sunday church services were an absolute must for Victorian and Edwardian families and as the local churches could not accommodate the masses arriving each Sunday, the Pier was opened—free of charge—for services conducted by the various ministers in the town in turn. Having satisfied this moral obligation, trippers felt free to shake

Dense crowds on the North Pier in the early years of the twentieth century. In its early days the pier was opened free of charge on Sunday mornings for holidaymakers to take part in religious services conducted by the town's clergymen and ministers in turn.

off the dust and grime of their home town and the restrictions of decent behaviour and to have "a hell of a good time".

So popular was the Blackpool Pier that soon another pier company was formed, oddly enough—as it appeared to be in competition with the first pier—by the same directors. This second pier was to have been called the South Pier, although when yet a third pier was built the second pier was re-named the Central Pier. The entrance to the Central Pier opposite the *Wellington Hotel* was built on land owned by Robert Bickerstaffe, who offered it to the pier company free of charge. Robert probably hoped the second pier would bring a great many visitors to his hotel, but when it opened on 30th May, 1868, it did not prove to be as successful as the first pier; far from the pier benefiting the *Wellington Hotel*, Mr Bickerstaffe had to prop up the finances of the Central Pier with the hotel takings. It was his nephew, young Robert, who lifted the new pier out of the doldrums by making it attractive to

the working classes with its outdoor ballroom, which resounded to their heavy stamping as they danced to all the popular tunes of the day, while the North Pier continued to concentrate on concerts for well-to-do visitors. And young Bickerstaffe's experience as lifeboat coxswain and his knowledge of the Fylde coast stood him in good stead when he incorporated a steamer service from the end of the pier which, like the dancing, proved enormously popular.

Other holiday attractions quickly appeared on the scene. The year the second pier opened an Arcade and Assembly Rooms were established in Talbot Square; the Assembly Rooms later became the Theatre Royal, Blackpool's first real theatre (now Yates Wine Lodge). Four years later in 1872 the Raikes Hall Park, Blackpool's most ambitious project to date, was opened. The park and gardens contained every type of amusement including a large theatre and concert hall, and many visitors spent the whole day there, leaving the grounds only when it was time to catch their train

Opposite page: The only traffic on the Promenade in the eighteen-eighties was horse drawn; this included the trams. On the right of the picture is Dr Cocker's Aquarium and Menagerie.

Left: The second Blackpool lifeboat and its crew. Robert Bickerstaffe was coxswain of Blackpool's first lifeboat, the Robert William, *and John Bickerstaffe was in the crew of the second boat, the* Samuel Fletcher.

home—to the annoyance of the promenade amusement caterers. Unfortunately the park and gardens were so far out of the town centre and away from the promenade and sea—in spite of the advertisements which said that the park was only 300 yards from either railway station—that the novelty wore off eventually; as their popularity waned they became a financial embarrassment to their owners.

A serious situation arose for the town when in the late eighteen-seventies the country suffered a severe depression; the number of visitors fell by nearly a third from over one million people a year to fewer than 700,000. Further depressed by a period of bad weather, receipts from all the entertainments in the town dropped to an all-time low. Something spectacular was clearly needed to bring the visitors back and also to extend the short summer season; that spectacular remedy was supplied by Dr William Henry Cocker, who hit upon the idea of illuminating the Promenade with the new electric light which was being used for the first time in some of Europe's

major cities. This was done by suspending huge arc lamps from 60-foot standards along the central beach; the current was provided by dynamos driven by traction engines.

The opening ceremony was held on 19th September, 1879; the project was so successful that visitors flocked in their thousands to see this "Wondrous Sight". For most people it was their first glimpse of the new electric light, and both piers did a marvellous trade with sight-seers wanting to view the "Illuminations" from a safe distance—no one wanted to be too close in case they exploded. The arc lamps cost £3,500, but as it was felt they brought business to the town worth far more than this the town council decided to continue them each autumn; it was not until 1893 that they were replaced by a larger number of smaller arc lamps.

The enterprising Dr Cocker was possibly Blackpool's first main showman, yet his background could not have been further removed from the brash, harsh reality of making a living in a growing seaside resort. Already a wealthy man when he retired from medical practice, he was later described by his great friend John Grime, editor of the *Blackpool Gazette News*, as "a brilliant man who seems to have the capacity to peer into the future".

Dr Cocker bought what had originally been Sir Benjamin Heywood's mansion on the central promenade between the two piers for £16,000 with the intention of offering it to the town for use as municipal offices, but the local board declined the offer, so for his own amusement he transformed the house and grounds into an aquarium, aviary and menagerie. He stocked the aquarium himself from his fishing expeditions, and at the entrance he placed an Orchestrion, a large automatic barrel organ which played all the popular classical tunes of the day. Dr Cocker opened it to the public in 1874, with gardens, bands, refreshment bars and stalls, which he let out to local traders for the sale of souvenirs. The enterprise was described in the guide books of the day in the following terms:

> The Aquarium, Aviary and Menagerie, seals fed at 11 a.m and 3.30 p.m, fishes at 11.30 a.m, and animals at 3 p.m. Selection by the Splendid Orchestrion, overtures, valses, marches and quadrilles during the day, refreshments, bazaars and fancy goods.

Finding it to be a great success, Dr Cocker set about expanding his enterprise. In the expansion the market stall holders were displaced, so he bought the adjoining Hygiene Terrace (later the site of the Palace) and transferred the stalls to this site, transferring also the name The Prince of Wales Arcade to this new building, which had shops and an Assembly Room. Later a theatre called the Prince of Wales Theatre was added and in 1881 a public baths and swimming pool was incorporated. In the long run none of these enterprises was financially successful; indeed, they made a hefty dent in Dr Cocker's personal fortune. He was able to bring financial success to the ventures he proposed for the town, but not to those he developed for himself.

Acutely aware of the need for more indoor amusement facilities, Dr Cocker decided in 1875 to provide an indoor alternative to Raikes Park, nearer the town centre. A company called the Blackpool Winter Gardens Company was formed with the doctor as chairman, and the search for a suitable site ended with the company buying Dr Cocker's house, Bank Hey, at the top of Victoria Street, for £23,000, which no doubt solved some of the good doctor's financial problems. For the opening of the new Winter Gardens on 11th July, 1878, Dr Cocker arranged a big parade and invited Mayors from nearly seventy towns to attend the opening by the Lord Mayor of London; all the civic heads were accommodated at the *Imperial Hotel* for the week at the improvident doctor's expense.

Like the North Pier, the Winter Gardens aimed to attract a higher class of visitors with cultural shows and orchestral performances, or that was so until the unfortunate Sarah Bernhardt affair. By the time the Winter Gardens opened the bulk of Blackpool's visitors were drawn from the working classes; many of the four thousand people who crowded into the new Winter Gardens to hear the famous actress were mill workers and their families. To everyone's surprise and disgust Miss Bernhardt spoke her lines in French; the acoustics of the Winter Gardens Pavilion were so bad that few people could hear her, and those who did could not understand the language, so she was mercilessly heckled. The disgruntled actress stalked out in high dudgeon before the end of the first act and refused to return.

The Winter Gardens management had to refund everyone's entrance money, to the delight of opportunists who quickly hopped from the cheap seats to the expensive stalls and claimed the higher price. Following this debacle the company instructed the management to avoid future cultural shows; many similar events in the town suffered a similar fate. The working classes were clearly not yet ready for a cultural education.

In 1880 Thomas Sergenson, who had been treasurer of the Prince of Wales Arcade, took a lease of the theatre for five years. Soon afterwards he also leased the Theatre Royal in Talbot Road, and under his guidance both theatres began to make a handsome profit, no doubt because of his policy of catering for the working classes with the type of show they could understand and enjoy. It was not long before Mr Sergenson announced that he was going to build an entirely new theatre in Church Street, nearer to the promenade than the Winter Gardens, and that he would call it the Grand Theatre.

This news alarmed the directors of the Winter Gardens, which had been doing badly for a few years. Following the Sarah Bernhardt disaster and against the wishes of Dr Cocker,

they appointed a London impresario, Bill Holland, who had previously been successfully managing a number of London theatres and music halls. Holland, who styled himself "the people's caterer", scorned the Winter Gardens' past policy of catering only for upper-class visitors and set out instead to woo the masses. In this he was highly successful; for some years the Winter Gardens regained their popularity and the receipts were gratifyingly high.

After all, wooing the masses was what Blackpool was all about.

Blackpool beach and the Promenade in Victorian times, before the building of the Tower.

Palaces and Towers   3

WHILE BLACKPOOL was wooing the masses of Lancashire and Yorkshire, London was impressing and beguiling the middle and upper classes with marvels of science and engineering; it was an age of innovation and invention.

New and impressive ideas for buildings were constantly being proposed, most of them so preposterous and outrageous in concept and design that few if any reached the building stage, and most of those that did foundered for lack of capital. London and Europe abounded with these short-lived enthusiasms; even Decimus Burton, Fleetwood's architect, was commissioned to design an amusement park which was to be larger than St Paul's Cathedral, but there is no record of it surviving beyond the drawing board.

Iron and steel increasingly proved a cheap replacement for masonry. The advantage of iron over masonry lay in the much smaller amount of material required and the speed of erection; soon it was being used universally for all manner of buildings. In Paris in 1849 it was used for a railroad station; two years later Joseph Paxton built the Crystal Palace in London for the Great Exhibition of 1851, using a form of cage construction with relatively slender iron beams as a skeleton for the glass walls of a large open structure, with diagonal rods providing resistance to the wind forces.

Two features are particularly important in the history of metal construction, first the use of latticed girders, a form first developed in timber bridges, and second the joining of wrought-iron tension members and cast-iron compression members by means of rivets inserted while hot, thus giving the structure strength and resilience. The development of the Bessemer and Siemens-Martin processes in the eighteen-fifties and eighteen-sixties opened the way to the use of steel for structural purposes. The Crystal Palace was certainly an imaginative and ambitious use of the new materials, which pleased and delighted not only the Victorian public but also the Exhibition's patrons, Queen Victoria and Prince Albert. And if there was anything the Victorians liked more than an English scientific marvel, it was a building so impressive that even its continental contemporaries were jealous. For a time Londoners happily basked in the glory of the Crystal Palace until, to their extreme annoyance, they heard that Paris was proposing an Exhibition—or Exposition as it was to be called—of their own to commemorate the centennial of the French Revolution. Interest was caught, however, and irritation increased, by the announcement that Monsieur Gustav Eiffel had been commissioned to build a "suitably symbolic structure" for the occasion; he said it would take the form of a tower which would be the tallest building in the world.

The building of towers has always fascinated man, perhaps prompted by an urge to leave his imprisoning earth and to climb into the sky. One of the earliest recorded examples of tower building can be found in the Bible—the tower of Babel.

Most early towers depended on stairs to permit access to the topmost part, but a combination of the invention of the powered lift by Elisha Graves Otis in 1861 and the increasing popularity of iron and steel as a building frame probably inspired Gustav Eiffel in his choice of materials and design for his building, which would eventually bear his name. Steel had been used by Eiffel before; indeed, he was a leading bridge engineer who had made his name with the use of metal pylons to carry viaducts and with the iron framework supporting the Statue of Liberty in New York. Yet when he put forward his proposal for a 300-metre tower of iron and steel he was opposed by artists, architects and engineers on the grounds of expense, aesthetic appearance and uselessness. In an age of excessive floral decoration on everything from furniture to buildings, his clean, straight lines with no curlicues were deeply offensive to the aesthetic senses of the mid-Victorian era; the arguments were never-ending and completely indecisive. Most Parisians, however, realised this new tower would be something they could be proud of, something no other nation had. To this day it is claimed of the Eiffel Tower that it is the most loved and the least lovely of Paris monuments.

It was ultimately announced that the Tower had cost as many gold francs to build as the number of kilograms it weighed, 5,600,000, or in English money £298,000, which even for those days was a very slight amount for such a project. Owing to the weight of opposition building was delayed until nearly the last minute; it was erected in an astonishingly short time, and was ready for the opening of the Exposition in 1889. As it was erected it was joined piece by piece by three hundred acrobatic riveters, its slight weight of 7,000 tons being held by concrete piers sunk into the ground; in all there were two and a half million rivets holding 12,000 metal struts.

The area between the four legs is more than two acres, yet it is calculated that the structure exerts no more pressure per square inch than a man seated on a chair. Originally 984 feet high,

the Tower was increased to 1,058 feet by the addition of a wireless mast; the height varies with changes of temperature by about 15 cm (6 inches).

The powered lifts which the Otis Elevator Company fitted ascended on a curve because of the design of the legs; an added attraction was that they were glass cage machines, enabling their passengers to enjoy the breathtaking views during the ascent.

It was undoubtedly the tallest building in the world, more than double the height of the Great Pyramid, and it remained supreme until the erection of the Chrysler Building in New

York in 1930. The crowds who flocked to the 1889 Exposition to see it were given the ability, which no man had ever had before, to see their own capital from a magnificent vantage point, and the cost of the Tower was recovered in a relatively short time.

It was originally thought that the Tower would have only a twenty-year life and would be demolished in 1909, but when that date arrived even those who had opposed its erection were vociferous in their demands that it remain.

In London the challenge of the Eiffel Tower had to be taken up. The man who accepted this challenge was Sir Edward Watkin. In 1889 he formed the Metropolitan Tower Construction Company with the purpose of building a tower which would be even higher than the Eiffel Tower. He acquired 280 acres of land in Wembley and decreed that this would be not only the site of his new tower but also a vast outdoor amusement park to which visitors would travel by rail; as he was the chairman of the Metropolitan Railway Company as well as of the Tower Construction Company there would be no difficulty about arranging for a railway line to the new amusement park.

It is perhaps fortunate that this tit-for-tat attitude did not continue or the two countries might, today, be dotted with towers of increasing heights, serving little or no useful purpose. Fortunately, the god of finance kicked the whole idea into touch, for the Wembley Tower was never completed, the money running out early in its life. A competition for designs for the proposed Wembley Tower produced some quirky and preposterous ideas from noted engineers and architects. One would have been a perpetual monument to vegetarianism, with vegetarian families living in the structure and growing their own food in gardens placed strategically in the tower. Another was actually called the Tower of Babel and was cone shaped, coming to a sharp point and having an outside spiral gradient for a train to take passengers to the summit.

The design which won the prize and was accepted by the company was very similar to the Eiffel Tower, a tribute to Eiffel's design. After five years' work the Wembley Tower, which was to have been 1,150 feet high, had reached only 155 feet, and then the money ran out. The stump of the tower remained until 1907, more costly to remove than its value as scrap.

The Manchester firm of Heenan and Froude had been engaged for the construction of the Wembley Tower. Curiously enough, they had also been engaged on a similar project in the North of England. Indeed, their chief engineer, a Mr W. Gilbert, was brought from his work on the other tower to supervise construction of the Wembley Tower. By the time the Wembley Tower, or Watkin's Folly as it was to be known, was in its death throes the tower in the North of England was being born, but it was having troubles of its own.

Left and right:
The Wembley tower was to have been 1,150 feet high, but it reached a height of no more than 155 feet before the money ran out. As the picture on the right shows, it was intended as the centrepiece of a great amusement park.

The Tower is Born 4

THE SUCCESS of the Eiffel Tower had attracted the attention not only of Sir Edward Watkin. Many others had similar ideas of building towers of iron and steel, among them a London-based company calling themselves The Standard Contract and Debenture Corporation, who conceived the idea of promoting the building of towers at northern seaside resorts as communications beacons.

One was to be at Douglas, in the Isle of Man, but this progressed no further than the foundations, which were laid in October, 1890. Another was built at Morecambe but almost as soon as it was completed it began to subside, and it had to be pulled down; it is by no means certain that the Standard Contract and Debenture Corporation promoted that particular tower.

Where the others were to be is not clear, but one was certainly proposed by the London-based company for Blackpool, which in 1889 was a growing and lusty seaside resort and already attracting more than its share of Lancashire and Yorkshire holidaymakers. The Winter Gardens had just opened its new Opera House, a move which proved popular with everyone except Dr Cocker, who resigned from the board in protest.

Dr Cocker's snobbish attitude was heartily endorsed by his friend Mr John Grime, who repeatedly declared through his newspaper columns how regrettable it was that the common people were driving away "their superiors and betters". The suggestion of a tower for Blackpool, therefore, received a very mixed response. The tower was clearly a gimmick to attract the masses, and the people who were being asked to interest themselves in the proposal were the old-time amusement caterers who still wanted to encourage wealthier patrons to the town. While some inland newspapers gave the idea every encouragement, Mr Grime was by no means enthusiastic, sowing doubt in many local businessmen's minds.

The Standard Contract and Debenture Corporation intended to find a suitable site, buy it, and then re-sell it at a profit (they were businessmen, after all) to a company which would be formed for the purpose of actually building the tower. Before very long it became obvious that the corporation was less interested in building a tower than in a spot of financial finagling over sites and contracts.

Out of a number of possible sites the corporation selected Dr Cocker's Aquarium, Aviary and Menagerie on the central promenade. For some years Dr Cocker's venture had been unprofitable and he had sold it to the Blackpool Central Property Company for £44,000. The sale included the *Beach Hotel*, the Market Hall and the shops, and the whole package was offered to the Standard Contract and Debenture Corporation by the Central Property Company for £60,000. The corporation then offered the site to the newly registered Blackpool Tower Company in 1891 for £95,000, giving themselves a satisfactory profit. They also negotiated for £30,000-worth of shares which they hoped to sell later at an inflated price, and they blithely underwrote the balance of the £150,000-worth of Tower Company shares which were offered to the public. Because of public misgivings and doubts fewer than two-thirds of the shares were taken up, virtually no Blackpool people showing any interest.

The five directors appointed were Alderman John Dickens, an ex-Mayor of Salford, Wilfred Anderton of Preston, Arthur Lowcock of Whitchurch, William Bratby of Hale in Cheshire, and John Bickerstaffe of Blackpool. John, of course, was the son of Robert Bickerstaffe, who had rescued the Central Pier from its early difficulties; as the only local man, he was made chairman of the new company, and on his shoulders fell the many early trials and tribulations encountered by the company. John was an ambitious and enterprising man but, despite his fervent belief in the ultimate success of the Tower, he must have spent many sleepless nights when the venture appeared to be foundering and everything he possessed seemed likely to go down with it.

With such a disappointing response to the share issue there was insufficient working capital, so when the foundations were laid and money was needed for the construction work the Standard Contract and Debenture Corporation were called upon to honour their underwriting and supply the necessary cash. No cash was forthcoming.

As chairman of the Blackpool Tower Company John found himself facing his first crisis. The site had to be paid for, the architects had to be paid, the company laying the foundations needed money, and the builders of the Tower itself would soon be wanting payments; was the whole project to be stillborn, like so many similar schemes, for lack of capital? Were his pessimistic Blackpool colleagues who had refused to have anything to do with the scheme right after all? With the courage, determination and initiative which all his family had always shown, particularly in the teeth of adversity, John first haggled with the Standard Contract and Debenture Corporation, knocking down their price for the site to £72,000.

And as the corporation were unable to fulfil their obligation of underwriting the balance of the share issue they had to agree to forfeit their £30,000 shareholding.

Having effectively disposed of the parasitical London-based corporation, John found himself at the helm of a wholly northern—if not Blackpool—based company. The immediate problem was to find enough cash to get the Tower off the ground. He demonstrated his own confidence in the future success of the Tower by constantly increasing his own share holding, even to the point of selling his interest in other properties and ventures in the town and re-investing the money in the Tower, and his confidence did have the effect of influencing some local people to take shares in the company. The quotation for the foundations

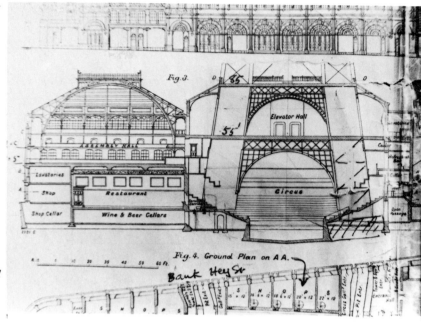

Left: Sir John Bickerstaffe
wearing the sailor's cap
which he continued to
wear throughout his life, a
reminder of his family's
seafaring traditions.

Right: Technical drawings
of the Tower buildings still
in the possession of the
Blackpool Tower
Company.

was £3,000, and that for the Tower buildings was £42,000, excluding the lifts, but this would only be the start; a great deal more money would be needed. The lift installation would cost quite a lot, and the Tower buildings had to be furnished, decorated and staffed, and John knew that the final bill would be vast. He knew that if the enterprise failed the town itself would be irrevocably damaged.

Five major firms, with a consultant engineer and a number of local subcontractors, were involved in the construction of the complex. The architects were Maxwell and Tukes of Manchester, and they engaged a Mr R. J. G. Read of Westminster as consultant engineer; he had considerable experience, both in England and overseas, of similar iron and steel structures. Messrs Heenan and Froude, also of Manchester, were the contractors for the Tower buildings while the contract for the erection of the Tower itself was let out to Mr J. Bell of Formby, the actual work being carried out on the spot by Mr W. Bell and Mr J. Wilcox, while the foundations were laid by Robert Neill and Sons of Manchester; the

sub-contract for the buildings went to James Cardwell and Brothers of Blackpool.

Maxwell and Tuke, who had also designed the Manchester Royal Jubilee Exhibition in co-operation with Messrs Heenan and Froude, had very carefully checked all their calculations to ensure the building would withstand the forces to which it would be subject, for Blackpool's gales were well known. The whole concept was very carefully thought out and all the firms concerned studied at great length the techniques involved in other steel and iron structures in general and the Eiffel Tower in particular. Great importance was given to the size and positioning of the supporting legs, safety and endurance being the two major factors; there must be no possibility of subsidence or collapse. Attention was also paid to fireproofing the whole structure, a matter which is still of prime importance to the present management. Monsieur Eiffel was invited to come to Blackpool to supervise the construction of the Tower, but the invitation was declined.

The site chosen for the Blackpool Tower was

21

Left: *The base girders of one of the Tower's four legs set in position on top of the concrete foundations.*

Below: *The concrete foundations of one of the legs, with the bolts to hold down the base girders already set in place. The tops of these bolts can be seen in the picture above.*

The base of the tower under construction in 1892. The complicated steelwork of the legs is seen to advantage in this view.

so restricted by the small amount of land available that the setting out of the foundations had to be very carefully considered, but by midsummer of 1891 work was well under way. The centre point was marked by a brass plug in a 12-inch by 12-inch pitchpine block fixed in concrete; over this was built a hollow brick pier 20 feet high with a plate and screw adjustment for mounting a theodolite, surrounded by timber scaffolding (all this in what is now the circus ring). From this centre point the position of each leg was determined.

The legs were then sunk in an elaborate foundation of boulder clay, concrete, and steel grillages to distribute the weight (full technical details and drawings of the foundation and the tower are given in an appendix).

Over the decades a curious myth has grown up in Blackpool about the Tower foundations. It was prompted—with a mischievous glint in his eye—by John Bickerstaffe himself; when asked what the Tower was built on, he replied: "Bales of cotton, lad, bales of cotton". He was, of course, speaking figuratively, thinking of the thousands of Lancashire cotton workers without whom the Tower would not have survived, but Blackpool landladies for many years assured their visitors that the Tower was

indeed resting on bales of cotton.

The circus is set between the four legs and provision was made for a gallery around it at a height of 20 feet above the ground. Patrons who are aware of their surroundings can enjoy the astonishing sight of the four gigantic legs tapering up and around the ring, with the elaborate iron and steelwork covered profusely in gold leaf, giving the whole arena a uniquely beautiful appearance. Surely no circus performance in the world takes place in such an amazing setting?

The ceiling of the circus forms the floor of the elevator hall at the 55-foot level. The elevator floor is made of concrete between rolled steel joists resting on girders; from this floor start the lifts which rise straight to the top platform.

As the foundation building was completed and the tower began to rise, some form of communication between the men on the ground and men working on the tower was needed; this became more urgent with each increasing foot of height. A Heath Robinson affair was set up consisting of a speaking tube with a combined mouth/ear funnel at either end and a loud bell which was rung when anyone wanted to use the communication tube.

Fascinated visitors watched the growth of this strange structure, suitably impressed by the published figures and statistics: that over five million bricks had been used in the building, that the original weight of steel used was nearly 2,200 tons, that nearly 100 tons of cast iron was used, and that when completed the Tower would be 500 feet high.

The foundation stone was laid on 25th September, 1891, by Sir Matthew White-Ridley, Blackpool's MP. His words were recorded—presumably beforehand—on a phonograph cylinder which was placed under the foundation stone along with coins and newspapers. The Mayor and Mayoress of Blackpool were there, of course, but then John Bickerstaffe was Mayor that year; otherwise there was little local interest in the event.

To provide some daily income (after all, the visitors were already there gaping at the growing building, why not exploit them?) Dr Cocker's stock of fish, animals and birds with their tanks and cages was bought for £4,000; the doctor was no doubt glad to be rid of them. As Dr Cocker had by this time resigned from the board of the Winter Gardens due to a disagreement with them he might well have been secretly amused at helping the Winter Gardens' main competitor. For good measure he threw in the popular Orchestrion. As the Tower began to rise like a huge Meccano set, the Aquarium and Menagerie remained open to the public, and already souvenirs of the embryo Tower were available for sale in the Aquarium.

Despite gloomy prognostications by local businessmen and constant objections that the Tower was being built on one of the most valuable sites on the promenade and was ruining the long sweep of the beach, the structure continued to grow. By 1893 no less

BELOW this TABLET is the FOUNDATION STONE Laid on the 25th September 1891 by SIR MATTHEW WHITE-RIDLEY BART MP

than 1,100 tons of steel out of an estimated 2,200 tons had been used, and by then the old buildings of the Aquarium had been demolished so that work could continue on the new buildings.

Although by the end of 1893 the Tower itself was finished and had a new Union Flag flying proudly from the flagstaff at the top, the foundation buildings were far from ready. Despite John's brave announcement that the Tower would be opened to the public on Whit

Monday, 1894, he was having grave doubts about the wisdom of sticking to this date, but time was money and there was simply not enough money to carry out further work without an income of some sort. The only solution was to open the Tower on the specified date and to continue with the work at the same time, using the takings from the Tower as ready money. The Otis Elevator Company installed the lift system in good time, the Aquarium was ready on the ground floor just inside the entrance, with the Menagerie alongside it (it was later removed to another floor), and the Pavilion on the second floor was more or less finished, though not finally decorated. The circus ring with its water tanks and sinking floor for the water spectacle was also ready for the opening week, and with this both John and the public had to be content.

In addition to the circus performers, a regimental band and an orchestra under the direction of Mr Oliver Gaggs were engaged to play in the partly finished pavilion. Advertisements were placed in provincial newspapers and in the local *Blackpool Gazette News*, and the week before Whitsun John toured the South of England with bags full of Tower programmes, distributing them freely everywhere he went, in railway waiting rooms, hotel lounges and even the House of Commons. As a result of all this publicity shoals of inquiries were received by the *Blackpool Gazette News* and the Blackpool Tower Company themselves about an official opening ceremony; who would perform it and what time would it be? Plaintively and with obvious disapproval, the *Gazette* announced that there was not going to be an official ceremony, the Tower would simply be open to the public. They implied in veiled terms that as the Tower buildings were neither finished nor ready, the Tower was being opened far too soon.

But when Whit Monday arrived and thousands of eager, expectant visitors crowded the Promenade to see the new wonder and to queue to ride to the Tower top, John knew that despite everybody and everything the game was afoot; there was to be no turning back.

Opposition   5

A S THE century drew to a close Blackpool was rapidly becoming the premier Lancashire resort. With the opening of the Winter Gardens and Raikes Park and Gardens the town thought it had reached the pinnacle of its ability to cater for the masses, and most of the amusement caterers decided that the last thing they or Blackpool needed was John Bickerstaffe and his Tower. There were still the diehards who wanted to cater to the wealthy upper classes as well as the more down-to-earth progressives who wanted the lion's share of the cotton and woollen workers' hard-earned savings, and they all said the same: "We do not need a tower—the point is, will it do Blackpool any good?"

Each season battalions of cheerful cotton and woollen operatives headed for Blackpool, freed from their mill shackles and with fifty-one weeks' savings in their pockets. They were welcomed by smiling amusement caterers whose sole desire was to keep them happy, to empty their pockets, and to entice them back again the following year. The whole process was transacted in a beguiling and unashamed manner, and with the full co-operation of the holidaymakers, who wanted to enjoy themselves and to spend every hard-earned penny. The general feeling was that unless they had spent up by the time they left for home they had not had a good time; on the journey home the universally expressed sentiment was "I had a reet good time, I'm skint!"

Like it or not, the Tower was there. Despite the fact that it was the tallest building in the kingdom and the second tallest in the world, and that a record number of visitors came to see it on the opening day, there was still very little local enthusiasm for it. This was borne out by the grudging amount of space given to the opening day by the local newspaper run and edited by John Grime, who devoted four inches of print and a sketch to the event, admitting reluctantly that "attendances had been satisfactory". This lack of local interest was borne out also in the share market, Tower Company shares soon slipping to the bottom of the league in comparison with other Blackpool ventures; on the opening day Tower shares were listed at eighteen shillings for £1 shares.

There were plenty of pessimists in the town who foretold that the novelty would soon wear

off and the Tower would become another white elephant; no doubt this was a hope sincerely shared by those Blackpool amusement caterers who were badly hit by the new attraction. The Tower's first advertisement in the *Gazette News*, which stretched the full length of the page (21 inches!) and used every superlative in the book, was flanked by equally flowery inducements from rival establishments to patronize them instead, and for that season at least the Blackpool visitor had a dazzling array of talent and amusement to choose from. Everything the Tower advertised was capped by all the other enterprises, and the visitors were spoiled for choice.

The Victoria Pier had an "exceptionally strong" list of variety attractions, which included Mr De Jong's salon orchestra (Mr De Jong's son married the well-known musical artist Florence, sister of Ena Baga, the Tower organist). Bill Holland, "the people's caterer", offered with unblushing lack of modesty "The greatest show ever offered to the public . . . one continuous round of amusements, a Challenge to the World!!!" (This was more an oblique challenge to the Tower than to the world). He also took 21 inches to list "the

greatest show ever". And who could resist the blandishments of the Royal Palace Gardens (late Raikes Hall), who said of their programme: "Read it closely, for it is the Greatest and Most Gigantic show ever produced. At no place in the World can so much be seen for 6d". Unfortunately, few of these advertisements produced the desired results. For the open-air attractions Whitsun proved disastrous; the weather was cold and windy, and the lure of the Tower was too great. As Mr Grime sadly reported: ". . . the amount of business transacted in the oldest established centres of Blackpool during the Whitsuntide holidays has been far below the average".

For John Bickerstaffe the receipts from the first week were not only necessary, they were heartening, for on the first day alone over £2,000 had been taken. To get over their initial cash shortage and yet to provide essential services like bars, cafes, dining rooms and souvenir stalls, the Tower Company contracted out most facilities to independent vendors as and when the rooms were opened, but as soon as they were able to do so the Tower Company took them over for themselves. For the whole of the first season work continued even as the

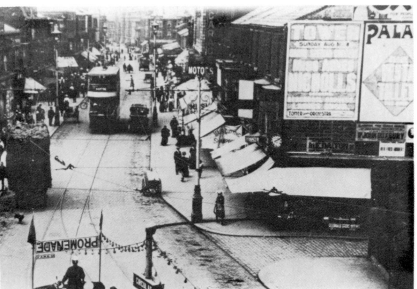

Opposite page: *A view of the Central Promenade and the Tower before the First World War.*

Left: *An early advertisement for the Tower, placed right opposite the Winter Gardens, one of the Tower's main competitors.*

visitors came, each month seeing the opening of another facility or service. Within the first few years temperance bars, cafes, lounges and even, as a result of the growing popularity of billiards, a billiard and smoking room appeared. For men only, of course; in those days ladies did not go into bars or similar male-dominated establishments.

Remembering the popularity of dancing on the pier as promoted by his uncle, John opened the Grand Pavilion—the hall in which the first day visitors had listened to concerts by a regimental band and the orchestra conducted by Oliver Gaggs—as a ballroom for dancing in the evenings; concerts in the afternoons continued to be given by the redoubtable Mr Gaggs. When news of the success of the dancing reached the Winter Gardens the management there were dismayed and annoyed; Dr Cocker had decreed that no dancing should

be allowed in the Winter Gardens, and to persuade him to revoke this order the company had to pay the hard-up doctor nearly £1,000, enabling them to offer dancing in the new Empress Ballroom, which they opened in 1896.

The Winter Gardens was, of course, the Tower's main competitor, and Bill Holland and John Bickerstaffe immediately engaged in a battle for supremacy. As fast as one produced something new and attractive the other tried to top it; the outright winners in the game were the lucky public, who always found something new and intriguing to tempt them. The two men adopted a policy of "anything you can do, I can do better". Bill Holland thought he had capped the Tower when he placed a large placard in a strategic position outside the North Station to catch the arriving visitors' eyes with "WINTER GARDENS IS THE BEST SHOW IN BLACKPOOL". The

The Theatre Royal in Talbot Square with its reading room. This later became Yates Wine Lodge; recently a music hall has been opened in the old theatre premises. At left is the famous fountain which disappeared long ago.

following day there mysteriously appeared at the bottom of this advertisement the terse but devasting words: "EXCEPT THE TOWER".

Others soon joined the fray. Before long advertisements for rival attractions were cheekily painted in bold letters on rooftops so that visitors ascending the Tower could look down and see them.

However reluctantly, everyone had to agree that the novelty did not wear off. The Tower's popularity went from strength to strength, and thousands of visitors flooded to the resort each year, attracted by nothing so much as the Tower. It was the ideal family venue in the regrettable event of a rainy day; and even on hot sunny days it would still be packed. Other attractions and venues suffered as a result. Raikes Hall and Gardens gave up the uneven battle in 1896, bought by John Bickerstaffe, who kept them open for a few more years before closing them down.

True to his promise, Thomas Sergenson started to build his own theatre in Church Street, engaging Frank Matcham to design and decorate it. With the title Grand Theatre, it opened two months after the Tower in 1894. It was a handsome and justifiably popular theatre, adding to Blackpool's lustre, but did not offer any serious opposition to the Tower. That is perhaps why when it became available in 1910 John decided to add it to the Tower's crown and purchased it for the company.

A more serious competitor was the ill-fated Alhambra Theatre, virtually next door to the Tower. The Prince of Wales Theatre and swimming baths, despite Mr Sergenson's efforts, had been a financial flop for more than twenty years when it was sold for £36,000, to re-open in 1899 as the Alhambra, the money being raised by public subscription. Intended as a rival to the Tower, the Alhambra had a 3,000-seat theatre, a 2,500-seat circus, a wax-works exhibition and a roller-skating rink; the whole conversion had cost as much as the construction of the Tower. Sadly, despite its prominent position on the promenade and despite (or perhaps because of) its proximity to

30

Building the "Gigantic Wheel" in 1896. Impressive though it was, the wheel was not a success and was dismantled in 1928 to make way for the Olympia building.

the Tower it was a dismal failure from the start, and within three years it was in the receiver's hands. For two years the Tower Company hesitated before deciding to buy it; they did so for £140,000, altering it and opening it in the name of the Palace—without the circus, of course. They changed the building considerably, incorporating a curious museum of oddities, bars and soda fountains, but they retained a very unusual item in the form of a moving staircase or escalator, the first of its kind and a great novelty when it had been installed in 1901; it had cost a penny to ride on it. The Palace was re-opened in 1904 and was for more than fifty years a great asset to the Tower Company's complex. An underground passage was provided between the two adjoining buildings in 1914, making possible the economic sharing of many facilities, including electricity. When the Palace was closed, to re-open as Lewis's store, the passage too was closed, and there is now no link between the two buildings.

In 1911 a cinema was incorporated in the Palace and during the nineteen-thirties an admission charge of a shilling entitled the patron to dance in the magnificently decorated ballroom and also gave him entrance to the "gods" of the variety theatre or the gallery of the cinema.

In 1896 Mr W. G. Bean opened what was later to be called the Pleasure Beach with his first bicycle ride; at that time nobody realised that this would eventually become one of the Tower's greatest competitors. Not that the Pleasure Beach worried the Tower Company a great deal at any time in its life, for it was mainly an outdoor attraction; when the weather was fine it throbbed with life, while the Tower came into its own in bad weather. Soon Blackpool was to count itself doubly blessed with these two major attractions.

As an alternative draw to the formidable Tower, Bill Holland at the Winter Gardens decided to build his own iron and steel structure, a "Gigantic Wheel". Second only to the Tower as a feat of engineering prowess, the wheel was erected in 1896 at a cost of £50,000. It was not initially the property of the Winter

Gardens, being built by an independent company formed for the purpose, but like the Alhambra the "Gigantic Wheel" proved to be a white elephant. Mr Holland was not to see the opening of the Wheel, for he died suddenly in 1895 before the structure was complete.

Built on the corner of Victoria Street and Coronation Street, it was by its very size impressive and imposing, but it was disappointing in action, providing nothing more exciting than a slow, jerky and uncomfortable ride. It languished in less than lukewarm popularity for twenty years before the Winter Gardens Company took it over for a mere £4,000; they found that the cost of dismantling the Wheel was greater than its scrap value, and it was not until the Tower Company took over the Winter Gardens Company in 1928 that the Wheel was demolished to make way for the Olympia building. Most of the girders and stays were sold for scrap, but some of the metal was used to produce medals which were sold for sixpence each. The spindle or axle was more than 40 feet long, weighed over 29 tons and had a diameter of 24 inches. The coaches were all sold for £20 and £30 each; some still remain around the Fylde countryside, used as hen cabins, bus shelters and a popular cafe which

provides a sad reminder of a once-proud feature of Blackpool's skyline.

In 1895 another very formidable rival reared its head less than fifty miles away. Perhaps it was one of John Bickerstaffe's programmes, scattered so freely about the House of Commons in 1894, that led Mr R. P. Houston, Liverpool's MP, to conceive the idea of building an Eiffel tower in New Brighton, a growing resort on the banks of the Mersey. Wasting no time, he purchased the Rock Point Estate for £30,000 and immediately contacted Mr Frank Maxwell, the Manchester architect who had drawn up the plans for the Blackpool Tower.

With his experience and knowledge of the Blackpool Tower, Mr Maxwell negotiated a completely different agreement with Mr Houston, who at this euphoric stage gladly agreed to Mr Maxwell's terms. They included not only the usual architect's fee but also a five per cent commission on all the construction work, including any amendments or alterations, even cancellations. This tricky commission arrangement was full of pitfalls; subsequently Mr Maxwell was to sue the New Brighton Tower Company for non-payment of his commission, unfair dismissal, and other sundry grievances, and in return the New Brighton Tower Com-

Right: *The wheel nearing completion in 1896. A better view of the Lancashire coastline could be obtained more comfortably by ascending the Tower than by travelling in one of the cars on the wheel.*

PROMENADE FROM NORTH PIER, BLACKPOOL

Left: *A view from the North Pier showing the "Gigantic Wheel" and the Tower, used to produce an Edwardian postcard.*

any was to claim that among other things Mr Maxwell had privately charged the constructors a commission which had not been in the agreement. Eventually the whole affair was settled out of court, but this litigation resulted in unwanted delays.

On its formation in July, 1895, the New Brighton Tower Company had less difficulty than John Bickerstaffe in finding investors, probably benefiting from the success of the Blackpool Tower's first season which John had publicized in the hope of gaining local interest in his shares. Mr Houston raised his £30,000 for the purchase of the estate fairly quickly and was soon on his way to raising a second £30,000. His plans were ambitious. He intended laying out the 35 acres of the Rock

Point Estate as an amusement park, with floral gardens and the largest athletic grounds in the country.

The New Brighton Tower Company soon announced that their general secretary would be Mr R. H. Davey, who had occupied a similar position with the Blackpool Tower Company. As John Bickerstaffe had regarded both Mr Maxwell and Mr Davey as friends as well as business colleagues, he might have wondered who were his friends and who his enemies.

Work on the grounds of the Rock Point Estate—soon to be renamed the New Brighton Tower Grounds—started immediately on the formation of the company, but it was two years before the announcement came that the grounds would be open to the public, at Whitsuntide, 1897. The grounds were by no means ready, but, as at Blackpool, to avoid the loss of a whole season it was decided to go ahead with what was available. The weather on the opening day was, to say the least, unkind; rain poured down in torrents all day. Despite this, between thirty and forty thousand people paid to enter.

The visitors were disappointed that there was no special opening ceremony, and they were even more disappointed to find that the much-vaunted tower itself was little more than half built, and even the athletic grounds were not finished. One reason for the delay in building the tower was Mr Maxwell's difficulty in getting his plans accepted by the local council, who turned them down in June, 1896, and did not accept them for more than six months. This meant the foundations could not be laid until 1897, making it impossible to have the Tower ready for the published date. It was in fact two years before the tower was finished.

As with all the other tower projects, money became a problem; everything seemed to cost more than originally quoted for, and with the constant changes and alterations made by the directors another share issue had to be made. Even with this injection of capital, many of the original ideas as well as the new ones had to be scrapped.

Construction was undertaken by a Derbyshire firm, using much local labour, and extra men were taken on in an endeavour to complete the work to schedule. In all there were 3,500 men working day and night, which compared to Blackpool's 170 construction men seems excessively high and probably accounts for much of the extra cost. As a result of using this large workforce the tower was completed in twelve months, compared with Blackpool's three years, but the cost of the work was not counted merely in cash terms. Three men were killed and many injured, two of the deaths occurring within a fortnight of work starting. The clerk of works, who had also been clerk of works for the Blackpool Tower, eventually announced that although not completely ready the tower would be opened to the public at Whitsuntide, 1898, just a year after the opening of the grounds.

Despite another cold, wet day the grounds were packed and people queued to go into the tower buildings. To their intense disappointment the lifts had not been delivered and no ascents were possible; what use was the tallest tower in the country if you couldn't go to the top of it?

The New Brighton tower's height was, without the flagpole, 576 feet 6 inches. It had six platforms, four of which could be reached by a

The New Brighton tower seen from the River Mersey. Taller than Blackpool Tower, the New Brighton tower had a relatively short life, being demolished between 1919 and 1921.

staircase, and a large copper ball at the very top into which the flagpole was secured. Constructed of mild steel of British manufacture, it contained only 1,760 tons of steel compared to Blackpool's 2,200 tons and the Eiffel Tower's 7,000 tons.

Octagonal in shape, it had eight legs with a base 150 feet across and was more slender and lacy-looking than its sturdy counterpart in Blackpool. The building at the base of the tower had originally been designed like the Blackpool Tower building to have a circus between the legs on the ground floor, but this was changed to a theatre seating 3,000 people. The first floor had a ballroom and restaurant, and the third floor housed a roof garden, with the lifts ascending from this level. These were not installed by Otis but were electrically powered lifts supplied by Easton, Anderson and Goolden Ltd, of Erith. It was intended that there should be four lifts carrying twenty passengers each, but only the first two were installed.

While New Brighton's tower certainly attracted the crowds initially, John Bickerstaffe and the Blackpool Tower Company found that it did not draw people away from Blackpool, attracting instead crowds from Liverpool and surrounding areas. Apart from the popular ballroom, the New Brighton grounds suffered much the same fate as the Raikes Park and Gardens in Blackpool had done.

Blackpool Tower had a five-year start and its proprietors had considerable experience; it also had John Bickerstaffe at the helm. New Brighton had to admit that Blackpool was in a different league as a holiday resort, having the backing of many other major attractions for its visitors. Nevertheless, the New Brighton tower was a certain rival to Blackpool Tower.

The life of New Brighton Tower was relatively short, being virtually terminated during the First World War. Its popularity had been waning for some time, the ballroom remaining its main attraction, and years of wartime neglect resulted in an order to pull it down in 1919. The work took nearly two years; in 1921

Another view of the New Brighton tower. The buildings at the base had a longer life than the tower itself, surviving until 1969.

the last vestiges of the tallest building in the country were removed, leaving the ballroom buildings to continue for many years until they, too, were destroyed by a disastrous fire in 1969.

So after twenty-five years Blackpool Tower once again took its place as Britain's highest building.

Celebrations and Disasters 6

WITH the Blackpool Tower Company busy consolidating its position, each season brought some new improvement, some innovation.

Within a very short space of time there were four bars, refreshment rooms, dining rooms, restaurants with orchestras—sometimes as many as five or six orchestras were playing in various lounges, dining rooms, and the ballroom. The Tower included every conceivable type of indoor amusement and, with its ornate and opulent furnishings and decor, was a constant source of delight to the luxury-starved millworkers, liberated from their slavery for one glorious week at the seaside.

The furnishings and decorations were rarely if ever abused, damaged or vandalized. The Victorian working classes might have been rough and ready, but they were well behaved and most of them were quite content to stand and stare and wonder at this unbelievable luxury. To people who lived mainly in grimy towns in poor housing conditions this was an exciting and glamorous world; John Bickerstaffe's "nimble sixpence" provided them with something to think about and talk about for the next fifty-one weeks.

The fact that they met their neighbours and workmates in Blackpool during their week's holiday in no way diminished their pleasure. On the contrary, in the Tower Ballroom on Saturday night they become one big, happy family with one aim in mind—to enjoy themselves. Each Saturday special excursion trains ran from towns in east Lancashire to Black-

pool's Central Station, the admission price to the Tower being included in the half-crown (12½p) fare. Who cared if, after a night's dancing in the Tower, your train home did not leave until 1.30 am, leaving you with a walk home from the station at three or four in the morning? That was the way to enjoy the weekend!

The Tower played its part in celebrating Queen Victoria's Diamond Jubilee in 1897. On 22nd June, Diamond Jubilee day, the Tower stayed open until 1 am to allow people to see the bonfires which were lit at 10 pm all along the coast in honour of the occasion.

One month later people might have been forgiven for thinking the Tower was continuing the celebrations as they stood on the Promenade and watched the Tower top blazing merrily, shining like a beacon across the same coastline. A short circuit in the primitive electrical wiring was blamed for the fire, which started at 11 pm and spread to the wooden decking on the top levels of the first two platforms. The lift had finished working for the evening and no-one was at the top, which was extremely fortunate. Soon the staff were trying to reach the top platform by the staircase in a brave attempt to deal with the blaze, the fire having put the lifts out of action. Three men reached the platform from the iron staircase, but in the dark, with red-hot debris falling around them, they had to give up their impossible task and leave the fire to burn itself out, which it did with surprisingly little damage. Some of the worst of the damage was caused by one of the lift counterweights, which fell when the cable was severed. In falling, it crashed through the glass roof and landed in one of the circus boxes, where it still remains; it was decided that the cost and effort required to remove the heavy counterweight was too great, and the box was simply sealed behind a wall of mirrors.

For the rest of the season the lifts remained out of action while repairs were carried out, the whole system was rewired and the platforms were refloored in concrete. A new safety system was installed, making it impossible for such an accident to happen again; a positive braking system now comes into operation instantly if a cable should break.

The following year the lift service was resumed, much to the relief of the manage-

The "limestone cave" decor of the Aquarium at the end of the nineteenth century.

ment and the delight of the visitors. For many years the lifts operated only six days a week; only in 1925 did they begin Sunday operation. The Victorians did not approve of trying to reach heaven by lift on Sundays.

As the nineteenth century came to its end the Tower was taking the shape it was to have for the next decade or so. The Aquarium was still located at the entrance and was popular with all ages, seats being provided for those who wished to enjoy the peace of the "caves" and to listen to the classical music played continuously by the Orchestrion. There were first-class restaurants with immaculately-dressed waiters and three-piece orchestras, and dining rooms with neatly-dressed waitresses. In the restaurant they served a five-course dinner for two shillings and sixpence (12½p) and in the dining room a three-course dinner could be had for one and sixpence (7½p). Did the poorer people not have the appetite of the wealthier patrons?

In the Ballroom Oliver Gaggs and his orchestra played every day and nearly all day for the enthusiastic dancers, and alongside was the Temperance Bar, which was later to become the Long Bar with as pretty a team of barmaids as you could wish to see; ladies did not go in there! In charge of the barmaids in the Long Bar was Mrs Ogden, who guarded her girls from the attentions of the customers with the ferocity of a lion defending her cubs. Next to the Long Bar was the Menagerie, with its far-from-fearsome animals, who nevertheless thrilled the somewhat nervous spectators, despite their heavily barred cages.

When the press of customers in the Long Bar encouraged hopeful pickpockets to reap a rich harvest from the visitor's bulging wallets an attendant would appear and shout "Lion loose!" This had the effect of clearing the Long Bar in record time, thus thwarting the pickpockets.

Next to the Menagerie was the Monkey House, inhabited by, among others, the ever-popular Jacko, a baboon who never tired of displaying his repertoire of tricks and mischief to the delighted crowd.

The team of barmaids working in the Long Bar in 1898. Mrs Ogden is in the middle of the group and the lessee of the bar is standing on the left.

The roof gardens were a source of pleasure and delight to the ladies, who were encouraged to sit in cool, shady corners on comfortable seats and to relax among the magnificent and colourful plants. For those who had never seen anything more exotic than Aunt Bessie's aspidistra these were sights to marvel at; real palm trees, vines and floral plants of every kind and colour. And there was an orchestra giving concerts here every afternoon.

On the same floor as the roof gardens was "Ye Olde English Village"; if it looked like no English village anyone had ever seen, well, what did it matter? From here you could buy souvenirs and presents to take home for a penny or twopence. And from this floor, too, you could take the lift to the top of the Tower; the fare for the lift ride had been reduced to another "nimble sixpence". Not that you needed to be nimble to go to the Tower top, as

John was quick to point out in the programme; you needed only the effort to get into the lift and out again. Victorian ladies were given to walking, not climbing.

Above the "Olde English Village" on the west side was a staircase leading to a balcony with outdoor tearooms, a view of the bearpits—for the "animals who needed the open air", said the programme—marine views, and a promenade. All very pleasant on a warm, sunny day—and quite high enough for those of a nervous disposition, without going to the very top.

The proximity of the Central Station to the Tower—it was "nobbut a spit and a jump away"—resulted in a regular pattern for the holidaymakers. Immediately on arrival, while Mum and the kids waited with the luggage, Dad would nip along to the Tower and queue for tickets for the circus, for which the circus director had scoured the world to book the best in animal and acrobatic acts. After booking Dad would rejoin the family in the station and they would all set off in search of a week's

Left: *The Menagerie and Monkey House at the beginning of this century, from an illustration in the official programme and guide of 1903.*

Below: *The Roof Gardens in which visitors could enjoy the sight and smell of exotic plants even when the rain was pouring down outside.*

A later view of the Menagerie, showing the raised seating from which nervous visitors could study the animals.

lodgings. At least one full day would be spent in the Tower; the weather would decide which. Good days were spent on the sands or the Pleasure Beach, while cold, wet and windy days took the crowds flocking to the Tower. When the weather turned rough the staff would remark with a knowing grin, "I see Mr B's had his prayer mat out again!"

At the turn of the century the Boer War was occupying everyone's attention, even if wars and disasters did not in those days have the immediacy they have today. The Relief of Ladysmith and Mafeking brought great rejoicing to everyone, for it not only meant that many brave men were rescued but it meant, too, a return to the nation's pride in itself, and when news came of the fall of Pretoria the people's delight knew no bounds. On each occasion the town was bedecked with flags, and to mark the victory at Pretoria John announced that the Tower would hold a celebration concert to which admission would be free, the Tower being opened for the day without charge. Nearly eight thousand people took advantage of this opportunity to display their patriotism; no doubt this philanthropic gesture on John's part was more than repaid in

bar takings from the enthusiastic crowd.

Following the Wright Brothers' successful flight in 1903 the whole idea of powered flight began to catch everyone's fancy, and in 1909 Lord Northcliffe, owner of the *Daily Mail*, wrote to Blackpool Council proposing a flying display or Air Pageant, with cash prizes for the aviators who could fly further—faster—higher—slower—or even at all. As such an event would obviously be a great visitor attraction Blackpool received the idea enthusiastically, although there were a few doubting Thomases who predicted doom and disaster. The date was set and a site chosen (it was later to become Squires Gate airport) and in October, 1909, hopeful contestants arrived with their flying machines packed in boxes and crates for assembly on the spot. To Blackpool's disgust, the town was deprived of the honour of holding the very first air pageant in Britain; Doncaster beat them to it by a few days. But, the prizes offered at Blackpool being greater and more numerous, the cream of would-be aviators came to Blackpool. John offered £150 for the first man to fly round the Tower, but was forced to withdraw his offer on the grounds of possible danger to the surrounding

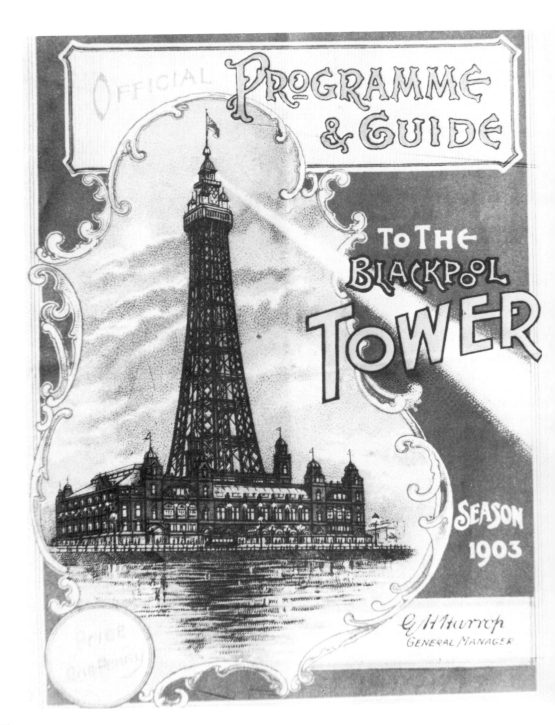

OFFICIAL PROGRAMME & GUIDE

TO THE BLACKPOL TOWER

SEASON 1903

G H Harrop
GENERAL MANAGER

Price
One Penny

Left: *The cover of the Official Programme and Guide to the Blackpool Tower issued in 1903.*

Right: *The Olde English Village on the same floor as the Roof Gardens, an illustration from the 1903 guide.*

Below: *The Tower Ballroom before the First World War. Trapeze wires and an "airship" can be seen hanging from the roof.*

A postcard issued at the time of the early aviation displays showed a variety of primitive aeroplanes apparently circling the Tower. In fact an offer of £150 for the first man to fly round the Tower had to be withdrawn in 1909 because there was thought to be too much danger to buildings and residents in the area.

buildings and residents. Undaunted, John offered a prize for the aviator who flew an all-British machine at least 100 yards without touching the ground. Well, aviation was in its infancy.

A series of flags was flown from the Tower top to indicate whether or not planes were flying that day, or even in the next hour or so. A red flag indicated that flying was in progress, a black flag showed that flying was definitely off for the day, and a white flag suggested that there might be flying if conditions improved. The pageant was a great success and Alderman Tom Bickerstaffe, John's brother, who was also a director of the Blackpool Tower Company, suggested that it be an annual event. For some years it continued to be held annually, and in later years aeroplane trips from Squires Gate round the Tower and back were very popular with intrepid visitors.

For those with their feet firmly on the ground life in the Tower went on, with John striving each year to improve it and add new attractions and ideas. By the beginning of the new century all the independent vendors had gone and the Tower Company were running everything themselves, with their own staff.

The unlikely "Olde English Village" had given way to an equally unlikely "China Town" which, with some alterations, later became an "Oriental Village and old China Tea House". Anything oriental was popular.

Stung by the Winter Gardens' new Empress Ballroom, with its lavish decor and resultant success, John closed the Grand Pavilion for remodelling and redecoration; it was reopened with a fanfare in 1899, delighting and entrancing the visitors who by now had come to expect only the most spectacular from Blackpool. The following year the same treatment was given to the circus, which was also remodelled and redecorated, but without losing the ever-popular sinking arena for the water finale.

Kaiser Bill and the outbreak of the First World War brought this programme of change and alteration to a temporary halt. Although the Tower did not close during the years of hostilities, it was fully occupied serving the dual purpose of helping the war effort and looking after each season's influx of war-weary visitors, mostly mill and textile workers now joined by a large handful of munitions factory hands. In 1915 fourteen thousand troops arrived in Blackpool, training mostly on the

44

sands and crowding into the ballrooms each night to relax and forget what the future might bring. Two years later the Americans arrived, creating competition—welcome or unwelcome, according to your sex—for the British troops.

The Empire and loyalty were on everyone's mind during the war, and each weekend found

famous speakers in the Tower doing their utmost to spur on the war effort. The speakers included Lady Randolph Churchill and the notorious Horatio Bottomley, who charged 100 guineas and said nothing worth hearing.

There were many patriotic concerts. One entitled "For the Love of the Mother Country" included a choir containing many local children under the direction of Pauline Rivers, with Dame Clara Butt as guest singer bringing down the rafters with her fervent rendering of *Land of Hope and Glory*. She was joined by a wildly cheering audience waving little Union Jacks supplied by the management.

In September, 1919, a Victory Ball was held to which everybody who was anybody came, resplendent in full evening dress after four years of near-austerity. Wounded soldiers of all ranks from the nearby Squires Gate convalescent camp gate-crashed the event—they had not been invited—and stayed as welcome guests.

As soon as the war was over Blackpool returned to catering for the masses who now wanted nothing more than to get back to enjoying their annual week's holiday at the seaside. Concerned about what neglect during the war years had done to the Tower, John immediately set about spending over £100,000 on the work of replacing corroded ironwork and repainting the whole structure from top to bottom. The lift service, closed during the war years, was resumed, the circus was redecorated, and a new entrance from Bank Hey Street was opened. One visitor complained that on a busy bank holiday the crush was so great that after paying his admission money at the promenade entrance he was slowly manoeuvred by the milling crowd through the doors into the Aquarium and out through the Bank Hey Street entrance without seeing anything!

A view of the Tower from the beach during the nineteen-twenties.

45

The Ballroom   7

THE GREEK gods are noted for their mischief, but surely their impishness surpassed itself when they cast the Bickerstaffes in the role of cupid. For nowhere does romance bloom more freely than on the dance floor, and in the second half of the nineteenth century the popularity of such intimate dances as the waltz enabled thousands of young people to embrace their loved ones first in the bracing air of the Central Pier and later in the soft lighting of the gilded ballroom. The popularity of dancing was such that both on the pier and in the Tower the floor would be full from the moment the doors were opened in the morning until the last waltz was played in the evening.

In order to equal, or preferably better, the Winter Gardens' Empress Ballroom John spared no expense. Frank Matcham, the noted architect who had designed Sergenson's Grand Theatre in 1894, was engaged to transform the Grand Pavilion, and for a year craftsmen including plasterers, gilders, and Italian artists worked to decorate the room in French renaissance style. When the work was finished it undoubtedly had a magnificence worthy of any Roman or Grecian ruler's residence. At the end of the room was a large ornate stage bearing the legend "Bid me discourse, I will enchant thine ear" on the proscenium, and over it was a large classical painting. John's own words may describe it best:

> Rightly described as the finest in Europe. It was a handsome room originally but it has been entirely remodelled and is now a masterpiece of the artistic in architecture and decoration. From the

spacious floor to the lofty ceiling, the interior coruscates with beauty. Commodious balconies, supported by massive pillars, surround it, and so extensive is the accommodation that seven thousand people can be seated comfortably. The decorations are in Louis XVth style and are surpassingly lovely. The ceiling is covered by beautiful paintings, the work of talented artists, and the paintings over the proscenium are brilliant in design and colour. The furnishing throughout is luxurious, elaborate and costly and altogether the Pavilion may be set down as perfect. The scene at night in the height of the season, when the mahogany, oak and walnut parquet floor—without rival from a dancer's point of view—is covered by hundreds of dancing visitors, while great crowds look on from the balconies, is one of surprising brilliance . . . one of the most popular innovations ever made by the enterprising management of the Tower is the provision of a sliding roof, 60 feet long, by means of which the interior can be kept cool in the hottest day in summer.

This description is by no means exaggerated. John told little more than the bald truth, it *was* magnificent, and even by today's sophisticated standards it is still an outstandingly beautiful place. When completed in 1899 the Tower ballroom was indeed one of the three finest in the country.

It was a typical Bickerstaffe trait to point out to the reader that it had been a costly venture, but who can blame him? Lighting was supplied by a series of small chandeliers; from the ceiling hung trapeze wires used by high-wire acts in the variety performances (the ballroom was used for concerts and variety turns in the

One of the huge chandeliers in the ballroom.

the accepted venue for every important occasion in the town. Before the First World War election meetings were held there, with John in the chair and guest speakers such as the Earl of Crawford and Balcarres, Lord Privy Seal in Lloyd George's coalition cabinet of 1916–18, C. W. Callis and W. G. Bean, and in 1906 the news of the great Liberal victory of that year was announced from there.

One of the first cinema films ever to be seen in Blackpool was shown in the ballroom. Brief and flickery, it was entitled "Queen of the North" and featured a ship steaming past the Central Pier jetty. When it was over, John sat back and said, "Marvellous, we are seeing history made".

And it was in the ballroom that famous people were given the freedom of the borough. In 1922, Lloyd George received this honour and in his speech of acceptance declared that Blackpool was a town of "dustless breezes". As such breezes provided a great contrast to the murky smoke-polluted air of the east Lancashire towns it was no wonder that the visitors liked to stand on the piers and promenade filling their lungs with the ozone-laden coastal air.

Many films have been made in Blackpool, most of them incorporating scenes in and around the Tower, always with the willing co-operation of the Tower Company. The first such film, "Hindle Wakes", made in 1925, is still regarded as a silent classic. Perhaps the best-known films were those made by Gracie Fields. One of the most recent is the life story of screen idol Rudolph Valentino, for which scenes were shot in the ballroom, using many local people as "extras".

To everyone's delight John Bickerstaffe received a knighthood in 1926, and to show their appreciation to the man who had devoted so much time and energy to the Tower the board of directors presented John with a three-foot-high silver replica of the Tower. It is on display in the Tower buildings today in the hall entitled "Memory Lane".

Sir John died only three years later in 1930, at the age of eighty. Surprisingly, considering

afternoons, dancing taking place only in the evenings until 1918). When it was later redecorated (in the original style) two large and elaborate chandeliers flanked by a series of smaller chandeliers were installed, making the room even more impressive, if that were possible.

The new ballroom received justifiable approval and was one of the most popular venues in the town. Mr Gaggs played to the enthusiastic dancers, and with everyone dressed in their best clothes under the soft romantic lighting an evening's dancing would, for most couples, be the highlight of their holiday. In many thousands of cases attachments lasting a lifetime were formed, and hundreds of the dancers today are the children or grandchildren of those who first met in the ballroom in those early days.

As if he had not enough to do, John Bickerstaffe acted as one of the Tower ballroom's first masters of ceremony, keeping a watchful eye on the floor to ensure that the crowd always flowed in the correct direction.

John was so proud of the ballroom that he encouraged its use for other events; soon it was

Right: *The midgets' wedding at St Stephen's-on-the-Cliffs, an event which attracted so much attention that a similar ceremony was introduced into the Midget Town performance at the Tower.*

Below right: *A silver model of the Tower presented to Sir John Bickerstaffe by the Tower Company directors in 1926.*

the amount of money that he must have had in his lifetime—his only indulgence was the occasional cigar—he left very little money, most of his undoubted wealth having been ploughed back into the Tower.

After his death his brother, Alderman Tom, became chairman of the company. He was equally devoted to the Tower and continued John's policy of constant improvement and change aimed at keeping the patrons happy. He brought the roof gardens up to date, putting in a waterfall and rockeries and installing large lamp clusters in the form of bunches of grapes just beginning to ripen (which are still there).

Adjoining the roof gardens there appeared a midget town, billed as "Fred Roper's wonder midgets and Argus the mind marvel". When two of the midgets fell in love and were married in St Stephen's-on-the-Cliffs Church, with tiny bridesmaids and attendants, the ceremony attracted so much attention that a similar ceremony was introduced into the Midget Town performance, using the same dresses but not always using the same couple. By the end of the season there were complaints that no one was sure who was married to whom.

With the retirement in 1929 of Mr Oliver Gaggs, who had been conducting orchestras in the ballroom, the circus and various lounges since the tower opened, many famous band leaders, conductors and orchestras appeared at different times in the Tower. The list is so long it would read like a "who's who" of the music world. Indeed, it became the ambition of all aspiring dance band leaders to play here, and those who did perform at the Tower included such famous names as Duke Ellington and Debroy Somers, Jack Hylton and Francis Collins, Ivy Benson and Mrs Jack Hylton. Larry Brennan, who had conducted famous dance bands all over the world, stayed for many years, and Sir Thomas Beecham gave afternoon concerts in the ballroom.

For the nightly cabarets the net was cast equally wide. Laurel and Hardy and Arthur Askey were engaged, with the Western Brothers, the Mills Brothers, and Richard Tauber (not all at once, of course); and at

Christmas and Easter there were concerts featuring music from *The Messiah* with massed choirs, and for most of these concerts the "house full" notice was needed.

During the thirties one of the most popular band leaders was Bertini, who started playing in the concert room of the roof gardens but was quickly transferred to the ballroom, where he reigned supreme until 1936. Bertini, who came from a very poor family in London, learnt music on a cheap violin acquired by his brother. Soon he saved enough to buy his own violin and with it ran away from home to find fame and fortune. He was gassed in the First World War, but he did not allow this to blight his musical career, and after many adventures joined the Gracie Fields and Archie Pitts organization. In 1928 he left them and came to Blackpool, obtaining work with the Tower Company. His melodic yet modern style of

music found appreciation among the dancers, and in many ways he endeared himself to his audiences.

One day, looking up to the balcony, he saw a row of small boys who by their dress he realized had come from a poor boys' holiday home in St Annes. As the band was playing a currently popular melody the boys started to sing and, hearing them, Bertini signalled to the band to play quietly so that the audience should also hear the boys singing; Bertini waved and smiled encouragement to them to carry on singing. To the surprise of the boys Bertini and the band arrived at the home the following day and to their delight they played for them for over two hours without any question of payment.

Bertini and his band broadcast regularly from the Tower. He claimed that the acoustics of the ballroom were so good that recordings

Right: *An advertisement featuring Bertini and his Broadcast Band.*

Opposite page: *The ballroom in which Bertini reigned supreme until 1936.*

Below: *Bertini and his band, with Charles Barlow on trumpet and Horace Finch on accordion.*

DANCE TO THE STRAINS
OF
BRITAIN'S FAVOURITE
RADIO DANCE BAND.

BERTINI AND HIS
BROADCAST
BAND Now Back at Their Original Home.

TOWER
2-30 —— TWICE DAILY —— 7-15.
ALL STATIONS
BROADCAST LATE DANCE TO-NIGHT.
DANCING TILL MIDNIGHT to
ORCHESTRA and WURLITZER ORGAN.

NO
EXTRA
CHARGE

General
Admission:
ONE
SHILLING

could be made direct from there without the need for a sound studio, and this was done for many years. His records sold in their thousands, and after each broadcast or record issue he received hundreds of fan letters.

Bertini left Blackpool in 1936 to tour the music halls. He died in 1952, still very popular. In his band of thirteen or fourteen, including three arrangers, were two men who were later to become famous in their own right. Charles Barlow later became the Tower ballroom band leader and was there for over forty years, and Horace Finch, who composed the music for Bertini's lyrics and was his pianist, became the organist in the Winter Gardens Empress Ballroom and made many records of his own.

What the BBC would have done in its early years without the Tower it is hard to imagine; sometimes there were as many as seven broadcasts in one day, and rarely a day and certainly never a week went by without a programme of organ, orchestral or dance music being relayed from there. In September, 1932, the Tower Company gave an order to the British Thomson-Houston Company for a public relay system to enable the Tower, Palace and Winter Gardens bars, lounges and ballrooms to hear the music as it was being played in the ballroom, thus obviating the need for different bands in the various lounges and giving the bar patrons the opportunity of hearing organ or orchestral music live.

Each winter the annual dances were tremendously popular; there were the Spinsters' dance, the Bachelors', the Medical Ball and the Benedicts'. With the ladies in glamorous evening dresses and the men in white ties and tails, a large floral arrangement and a fountain in the centre of the floor, coloured spotlights and a full orchestra, and with real rose petals being showered down from the ornate ceiling on to the dancers, these were never-to-be forgotten occasions. There were twenty-two dances with an interval for supper in the adjoining cafe with champagne, and after the interval the waltzes and foxtrots would quicken to charleston, turkey trots, and later jive and jitter-bugs. Just before Christmas

the Co-op held the Children's Balls, with admission 6d for each child; it is an astonishing fact that with over five thousand boisterous children attending there was virtually no lasting damage to the building!

By 1933 it was pointed out to Alderman Tom that after forty years' use by an estimated hundred million visitors the dance floor had been worn away by five-eighths of an inch and was in a bad way. Dancing styles had changed over the years, from the stately lancers and quadrilles to waltzes and two-steps and eventually to faster dances which took an increasing toll of the delicately sprung floor. The old floor was removed, the blocks were given to poor people as fuel, and a new floor of over 75,000 pieces of mahogany, walnut, maple and oak was laid during the winter months, dancing being transferred to the nearby Palace ballroom. When the last strip of flooring was in place there was a small private ceremony for the directors to inspect the new floor, and then they retired to "Sir John's Room", which had been opened in honour of Sir John Bickerstaffe, for refreshments. As the chairman, Alderman Tom, came into the room somebody whispered "My God, we're thirteen", and the speaker quickly left the room; ten days later Alderman Tom Bickerstaffe died suddenly of a heart attack.

During the winter of 1933 while the floor was

Right: *The ballroom with central floral display and fountains.*

Opposite page: *Removing the old floor of the ballroom in 1933.*

Below right: *Charlie Barlow, who had charge of the band in the ballroom after Bertini's departure.*

being relaid the ballroom had also been redecorated, still in its Louis XVth style but with some improvements in the balcony seating and lighting; the trapeze wires were removed and new chandeliers fitted.

New bandstands were installed, and a special stand for the new Wonder Wurlitzer which was expected. The first Wurlitzer, installed six years earlier, was transferred to the Empress Ballroom after being overhauled and enlarged; it was to be in the charge of Horace Finch, while the Tower's new wonder organist, Reginald Dixon, took over the latest arrival.

To celebrate the reopening of the dance floor there was a gala dance with Larry Brennan and his Band displaying their talents on the new bandstands. Two years later the popular Bertini left to tour the music halls, and after a time Charles Barlow became the resident band leader; he remained until he retired in 1978, after forty-six years with the company, having given pleasure to thousands of dancers in all three of the Tower Company's ballrooms.

But the Wurlitzer organs brought an entirely new style of dance music to the ballroom.

The Tower in the Thirties

Right: *A busy day on the Central Promenade, seen from the Tower top.*

Left: *Visitors looking at the animals in the Menagerie.*

Left: *The first class restaurant.*

The Wonder Wurlitzer 8

THE THIRTIES saw the arrival at the Tower of two new superstars, one a mechanical marvel and the other the wizard who manipulated it.

The *Blackpool Gazette* announced on 14th May, 1928:

> The first new Wurlitzer organ is now being installed in the Tower Ballroom. A gigantic Wurlitzer, the largest of its kind outside America, is being installed at the present time in the Tower ballroom. It cost approximately £7,000 and has necessitated the erection of a special organ chamber at the back of the stage. The organ will be used for recitals and dance accompaniment.

The organ had been made in Tonawanda, Illinois, America, where Wurlitzers were made until 1940. It was shipped across the ocean in thousands of pieces and reassembled in the ballroom by technicians who came with it.

On 17th June the *Gazette* reported again:

> The Wonder Wurlitzer was played in the ballroom for the first time today and is, to the ordinary person, a big box of magical tricks controlled by wizardry. It has every sound on it: cathedral chimes, sleigh bells, breaking waves, birds singing, fire alarms and even kisses are child's play to it. Once again Blackpool leads the field, for it is not only the best of its kind in the world, but it is the first ever to be installed in a ballroom. It has cost (with installation) £10,000.

And a further article described the new acquisition in some detail:

> It has fifteen miles of wiring, and thousands upon thousands of small connections; to count the numbers of small components that were needed in its assembly would be to run into millions. It is the only organ where the keyboard can move horizontally so that it can travel from the back to the front of the stage. It is an orchestra in itself, at the same time being more flexible than any orchestra could ever be. The organ includes 1,000 pipes, 1,200 magnets, two keyboards and 10 ranks of pipes.

Max Bruce, said to have been a boy prodigy, was the first organist to play the new Wonder Wurlitzer, which was first advertised in 1929 with him as the organist. Unfortunately, Max Bruce did not stay many months; it was obviously not an easy instrument to handle, and maybe it had not bedded itself in, but whatever the reason the following year it was advertised only as the new Wonder Wurlitzer,

Reginald Dixon
'Mr. Blackpool Himself'

I do like to be beside the seaside -

with no organist named. The Tower Company offered the position to Horace Finch, who was greatly tempted and felt sure he would have no problem taming this newcomer, but Bertini persuaded Horace to stay with him.

The Wurlitzer was proving itself rather difficult to handle, and with no settled organist on the horizon the Tower Company were somewhat disenchanted with their expensive new toy. That was the situation when a young man applied for an audition. He was a Yorkshireman from Sheffield who while on holiday for the day with his new wife had come into the ballroom, had seen the new organ and had chatted for a few minutes with Max Bruce, who told him the company were looking for a permanent organist.

That young man was Reginald Dixon. He had been born in Sheffield in 1904, and his first job had been as a cinema organist in the days of silent films; and he received the then princely sum of £3 a week. He had to improvise while watching the film with one eye and reading the music with the other in an effort to provide the appropriate sentiments, he recalled. One day he had a bright idea; removing the bottom from his piano, he was able when there was an explosion on the screen or the sheriff's posse thundered through the sagebrush for a shootout to give the strings a series of hearty kicks. "The effect", he said, "was terrific!"

Dixon considered himself a serious musician. In Sheffield he played in a variety of cinemas, one of which had the organ encased in a tank to protect it from the overflowing river. Another had a drunken projector operator, who often ran the films too slow, necessitating repeated adjustment to suit the music to the peculiar action on the screen. From Sheffield he went to Chesterfield, on to Dudley in the West Midlands and later to the Victoria Cinema in Preston, but he stayed there only a few weeks before a disagreement with the management resulted in his dismissal. Having just married his childhood sweetheart, he desperately needed a job—and then came his audition for the Tower.

At that audition, in March, 1929, he was asked if he could play dance music. He thought he could not, but he crossed his fingers and said "yes". In no time he proved that his unique style of playing was more than acceptable to the ballroom dancers.

With some reservations the Tower Company took him on for one season, telling him that if at the end of that time he was not suitable both he and the organ would be out. He started in May, 1929, and within a month was making his first radio broadcast; from then until Christmas he gave thirty-six broadcasts from the Tower ballroom on the new Wonder Wurlitzer. Never again was there any mention of dispensing with the organ or, for that matter, with Mr Dixon.

It is now a matter of history that Reginald Dixon not only tamed the mighty Wurlitzer but became one of the country's—maybe the world's—greatest exponents of organ music.

Reginald Dixon as he was seen by a cartoonist working for a local newspaper, the Blackpool Evening Gazette.

Reginald Dixon, the famous broadcast organist of the Tower, has made Blackpool renowned by his popular signature tune, now known all over the Empire.

His fame spread world wide. He received hundreds of letters, some addressed simply: Mr. Dixon, Organist, England. In 1933 he used a tune with which he was to be associated for the rest of his life, *Oh, I do like to be beside the seaside*.

Within four years he was sufficiently important for the Tower Company to accede to his request for a new Wurlitzer, built to his own specifications. A much larger machine than the original, with three keyboards and thirteen ranks, it incorporated a new carillon and an extra piano. Many people today believe the organ to be an electronic instrument, but it is a conventional pipe organ, with massive pipes and a large organ chamber behind the stage. In

the newly decorated ballroom an enlarged organ stand was built to house the new machine, and chief engineer Mr K. L. Foster and his son George fitted a new colour lighting console with a complete lighting system giving sixty-four different colours from four primaries. The original Wurlitzer was modified and enlarged to suit its new master, Horace Finch, and was transferred to the Empress Ballroom, where it delighted dancers for many years until eventually it was purchased by the BBC.

For five peaceful years Reginald Dixon demonstrated his prowess on the new machine, making hundreds of broadcasts and recordings. In 1940 he enlisted in the RAF and within two years was commissioned, serving as a staff

As a recording artist Reginald Dixon achieved considerable success. Here he receives a Golden Disc commemorating his achievements from Mr Ken East, head of EMI, in 1981.

officer and hoping against hope his hands would not be damaged in action, for without them he would be lost. Luckily he survived and in the fifties he was back again in his seat as the wizard of the Wurlitzer. Indeed, he had never really left Blackpool, for when he was on leave he used to sneak into the Tower and play for unknowing dancers, who had no idea that "Mr Blackpool" was playing for them.

With his famous signature tune he advertised not only the Tower but Blackpool itself. To show its appreciation the town invited him to switch on the Illuminations in 1966, and ten years later he went to Buckingham Palace to

Reginald Dixon with, left to right, Sir Joseph Lockwood, Lord Delfont, Dr George Badman and Mr D. Gledhill at the party which followed his retirement concert in 1970.

receive the MBE from the Queen, who told him she knew he was called "Mr Blackpool", adding "I often listen to you playing".

Although famous for his dance music, he remained a classical musician, and always accompanied the Christmas concerts and performances of *The Messiah*, which were, of course, broadcast. One broadcast was delayed by the howling of two cats; it was some minutes before they were found and caught. "Critics!" said Reginald, grinning wryly. A gentle, unassuming man who never lost touch with his public, he always endeavoured to comply with requests from couples who had danced to his music years before when they wanted something to remind them of their past.

Forty years after his first appearance at the Tower he decided it was time to retire; at the end of the season in 1969 he announced that it was his last. The Tower Company persuaded him to give one last retirement concert at Easter, 1970; it was a sell-out long before the date. The ballroom was packed with fans, many of whom had travelled not only from all over England but from abroad to hear the maestro for the last time; as the Wurlitzer console and Reginald Dixon rose into view the applause lasted for many minutes—and there were tears, too. The farewell concert was, of course, broadcast and was backed by the BBC Northern Orchestra and Vince Hill, but the audience had come only to hear their favourite organist. His final rendering of *Oh, I do like to be beside the seaside* brought the house down.

After the concert he was presented with a bouquet from the Theatre Organ Society of Australia, of which he was the Honorary President. The BBC presented him with a silver replica of the Tower Wurlitzer, and later Dr George Badman, one of the directors of the Tower Company, presented him with an inscribed gold watch on behalf of the Tower.

Although Reginald played occasionally for charities during his retirement he was glad to have the opportunity to travel and to do a few of the other things he wanted to do, but his plans were marred by the tragic death of his wife. In 1985 he, too, died in hospital, at the age of eighty.

A number of organists appeared on the Wurlitzer in later years, the youngest being Phil Kelsall, who took over from Ernest Broadbent. When Kelsall complained that the Wurlitzer was suffering from old age and needed some attention the Tower Company decided to have the work done regardless of expense. For three years the Wurlitzer was rewired and overhauled; the whole cost came to over £50,000, and it was not until 1981 that the Wonder Wurlitzer was back in service, giving pleasure to the thousands of dancers on the ballroom floor.

No one has yet replaced Reginald Dixon, perhaps nobody ever will. His memory will remain for many, many years, and hopefully so will the Wonder Wurlitzer.

Phil Kelsall at the Tower ballroom Wurlitzer.

The War Years 9

DURING the Second World War the Tower took on a number of new roles as Blackpool turned its attention from entertaining the masses to provide facilities for soldiers, airmen and others involved in the war effort.

The Tower top was taken over by the RAF as an emergency radar station. A 40-foot section of the spire was replaced by a wooden structure bearing the receiving aerials, and a number of steel cantilevers were inserted into the Tower at various heights to carry the transmitting aerials.

Many technical difficulties had to be overcome by the engineers and service personnel before the radar station could operate efficiently. There was interference from the tramway system on the Promenade, and even the steel structure of the Tower itself interfered with reception. The Tower Company's chief engineer, Mr K. L. Foster, worked night and day to solve the problems encountered by the RAF radar operators, whose task was to maintain surveillance of the Irish Sea from their eyrie at the top of the Tower.

The Tower top was also used as a lookout post by men of the National Fire Service and the Home Guard, and the buildings below were used both by the RAF and the Royal Artillery for training purposes. Blackpool had become a giant training camp, with more than 90,000 servicemen billeted in the town. The RAF used the ballroom and the Royal Artillery held lectures and training sessions in the circus each afternoon; in the evenings both ballroom and circus reverted to their normal role, providing entertainment both for the troops billeted in the seafront hotels and boarding houses and for the holidaymakers who came to Blackpool for a brief respite from aiding the war effort. Throughout the dismal years of war Blackpool's lamp of entertainment still shone brightly in spite of the black-out.

For the first six days after the declaration of war on 3rd September, 1939, all places of amusement had been compulsorily closed. The Tower staff kicked their heels, wondering what was going to happen. Then, realizing the value of keeping the nation's spirits up, the Government decided that theatres, cinemas and ballrooms could serve a more useful purpose open than closed. Blackpool immediately swung into action, training troops by day and entertaining them at night, along with the many visitors who crowded to the west coast.

Each evening every ballroom in the town would be packed with servicemen of all ranks dancing with local girls or visitors, many of them making a conscious effort to forget what the future might have in store for them. Many lasting friendships were forged, sometimes at the price of absent and temporarily forgotten sweethearts. The bands found a whole new range of tunes and a change of tempo for the dancers, *South of the border down Mexico way* and *Deep purple* giving way to *Run, rabbit, run, We'll hang out the washing on the Siegfried Line* and *We'll meet again*. And when the well-dressed and better-paid American troops arrived to sweep the girls off their feet, to the intense disgust of the poorly paid and drably dressed British servicemen, a whole new range of dances arrived with them.

As men enlisted or were called up, the Tower replaced many of them with women. The ballroom bands found their ranks depleted, many of them never to resume their former big-band status. When Reginald Dixon joined up he was replaced by a woman organist, the talented Ena Baga, sister of Florence de Jong, who took her sister's place when she was ill. Ena's signature tune was *Smoke gets in your eyes*, which became as familiar to the servicemen as Reginald Dixon's signature tune had been to pre-war holiday-makers. A newcomer to the ballroom band was Tommy Gaggs, grandson of the illustrious Oliver Gaggs.

Concerts were held in the ballroom to raise cash for "Salute the Soldier Week", "War Weapons Week" and similar campaigns. One such concert was given by the Hallé Orchestra, conducted by Sir Henry Wood, and another by the London Philharmonic Orchestra, conducted by Richard Tauber. In the Blackpool theatres there appeared all the big theatrical names as shows from London were transferred to the North of England.

Broadcasting from the Tower was a regular feature, both the Tower band and the organists frequently being heard on the radio in programmes designed to entertain the forces at home and overseas. The sound of the Tower Wurlitzer could be a reminder of better times and a boost to morale for a sailor in the wastes of the North Atlantic or an airman servicing a bomber in the Western Desert.

Near the end of the war Harold Grime, the editor-in-chief of the *Blackpool Gazette and*

Herald, while serving as an officer found himself leading a unit of Indian soldiers on to the stage of the Tower ballroom during one of the concerts. As the crowded audience rose and cheered them to the echo somebody whispered to him "Mr Grime, what would the national anthem of India be?" Puckering his brow, a perplexed Mr Grime whispered back 'Heavens, there are about a hundred and fifty of them." The band leader was by no means at a loss. The band struck up *Land of Hope and Glory*, which seemed to fill the bill quite adequately.

With the invasion of Europe people in Britain could begin to look ahead to the end of the war and to plan for a return to normal. The war years had brought a mixture of sadness and happiness to thousands of people as they lost relatives through the fighting or found new and lasting romance in the ballroom. Many Ameri-

can servicemen married English brides, and not a few returned home at the end of the war leaving broken hearts behind them.

But if the war had had its moments of tragedy, it also had its lighter moments, as when Lord Haw-Haw, a British broadcaster whose propaganda programme transmitted from a German station was listened to with amusement by many Britons, announced that the Luftwaffe had bombed Blackpool Tower, completely destroying it. It was even said that a picture of the Tower lying on the sands alongside the Central Pier had been published in German newspapers. To nobody's surprise the Tower was seen next morning in its usual place; one wit remarked that the Tower engineers must have been extraordinarily busy during the night getting it back into position.

With victory over Germany and then over Japan there began a slow return to normality,

Left: *A wartime dance in the Tower ballroom. Evening dances gave servicemen and civilians alike a chance to relax and forget for a short time the rigours of wartime life.*

Right: *The secret is out: the local press announces the Tower's wartime role as a radar station staffed by the RAF. An article from the* Blackpool Evening Gazette *of 15th August, 1945.*

THE *Best* VIEW OF THE ILLUMINATIONS IS FROM THE *Top* OF THE TOWER

500 FEET ABOVE THE "LIGHTS" AND THE PERFECT SPOT FROM WHICH TO SEE THE FULL BEAUTY OF THIS GLITTERING WONDERLAND

THE TOWER WILL BE OPEN ALL DAY......IF YOU HAVE LATE TRAINS TO CATCH YOU CAN SPEND HAPPY HOURS IN THE BALLROOM, MENAGERIE AND AQUARIUM.

CAFES AND SNACK BARS OPEN, where Meals are obtainable at all hours.

GENERAL ADMISSION 2/- (inc. Tax).

YOU NEED MAKE NO REAL WHILE'S MAKE FOR THE TOWER RESTAURANT OR THE WINTER GARDEN RESTAURANT OPEN ALL

WINTER GARDENS

With the blackout just a bad memory, the Tower got back to the job of wooing the masses. This post-war advertisement reminded visitors that if the trains did not leave until late at night or early in the morning, there was always plenty to do in the Tower.

and members of the Tower staff returned to familiar scenes as they were demobbed from the forces. The lift service, reserved for official personnel during the war, was restored to the public in August, 1946, and Walter Dutton, liftman for more than eighteen years, declared that he was delighted to see the public again. For six years he had taken RAF radar technicians and civilian firewatchers to the top; he had seen a German aircraft swoop in to bomb Seed Street when Blackpool suffered its only air raid of the war; and he had looked out from the Tower top at the flames as Liverpool blazed after the bombing of the town and the Merseyside docks.

When Reginald Dixon hung up his uniform and returned to claim his place at the Wurlitzer, Ena Baga moved back to London. She came back to Blackpool only to play at the new Odeon console for a Sunday concert, and on that occasion told a local reporter that her stay in Blackpool had made her famous in London; a common remark was "Oh, I heard you at the Blackpool Tower".

Blackpool was sorry to see Ena Baga go. She kept in close touch with the many friends she had made during her wartime stay in the town, telling them of her first television audition, which she found "exciting".

Plunging back into his work, Reginald Dixon returned to a round of broadcasting and making records; some of his records sold more than 70,000 copies, earning him a gold disc from the record company concerned.

He was vastly amused when one afternoon a dear old lady, evidently with no idea that she was talking to the organist, asked him "what time do they feed the animals?" "At 3.30", he said. "And what time does Mr Dixon play?" she inquired. "At 3.30", he said again with a smile. "Dear me", said the old lady, looking quite annoyed. "How silly to have both performances at the same time!"

And among his fan mail Reginald was delighted to have a letter from 71-year-old George Boyce, who told him that he was one of a dozen ornamental plasterers who in 1898 and 1899 had worked on the new ballroom.

The havoc wreaked by servicemen's boots on the floors of the ballroom and other rooms

An aerial view of the Tower in the years after the Second World War. The scene changed in 1962 with the demolition of the Palace, just to the left of the Tower in this view.

plus the enforced postponement of essential maintenance work during the war resulted in a spate of repairs when peace returned. The ballroom was closed for redecoration, and the opportunity was taken to make a number of changes in the general arrangement of the Tower buildings. The Menagerie and the Aquarium were both enlarged and the Oriental lounge was redecorated and refurnished.

The postwar years saw a period of austerity as Britain sought to repair the damage caused by five years of hostilities and to restore its shattered economy. With almost all the necessary materials in short supply progress was slow as Blackpool prepared itself for the holidaymakers who crowded into the town, glad to escape for a week or so from the restrictions of austerity and rationing. As many as 80,000 people regularly visited the Tower during the days of high summer.

By 1952 the whole town had been restored to a peacetime appearance and was enjoying something of a boom. So many people were coming to Blackpool on day trips to see the Illuminations that the town's railway lines were hopelessly congested at the height of the season. Some trains did not leave until 1 am or even 2 am, and the Tower Company was granted a licence allowing it to remain open until the last of the crowds had left for home. Reginald Dixon regularly remained at the organ console until two in the morning entertaining the tired trippers as they waited for the departure time of their trains.

Blackpool Tower still had its place in "a reet good day out".

Children in the Tower   10

BEFORE the First World War one of the seasonal attractions in the ballroom was an afternoon entertainment given by the Tower's own dance company, formed from local talent under the direction of Madame Pauline Rivers. At first it was a mixture of adults and children, but the children's performances proved so popular that soon they were appearing in their own show, billed as the "Blackpool Children's Ballet".

One extremely talented youngster whose name featured regularly in the programmes was the diminutive Emmie Tweesdale, billed as "Little Emmie", who appeared regularly from 1910 to 1935. Known as "La Petite Pavlova", she saw her picture appear on the covers of sheet music published under the banners of Horatio Nicholls, Francis Day Hunter, and Bert Feldman, and her fame spread far and wide beyond England to the Continent, where she had many fans and admirers.

Later she recalled that the children in the ballet were paid 3s 6d (17½p) per week, with extra for matinees. While the money might have been welcomed by the parents, the main attraction of being in the ballet was that it was a greenhouse for budding talents; over the long life of the ballet many of the girls went on to find fame and stardom.

The settings and decor were always lavish and spectacular, featuring a currently popular theme. During the First World War they had, as had all theatrical performances of the day, a strongly patriotic flavour. On one occasion

Little Emmie appeared suspended from the ceiling in an aeroplane; "I was the first to fly an aeroplane in the Tower Ballroom", she quipped later. This unusual performance was not without its disasters; on the first night the man operating the mechanism which lowered the aeroplane to the floor forgot his instructions and went home, leaving Little Emmie literally in the air. While a messenger dashed off to find him Little Emmie sang song after song to the still-packed ballroom until she was released from her perch.

Little Emmie retired after the death of

69

Dame Clara Butt, in the left-hand oval, and Pauline Rivers, in uniform in the right-hand oval, both took part in the patriotic show "For Love of Mother Country" in 1915.

PAULINE RIVERS
GRAND SPECTACULAR BALLET.
FOR LOVE OF MOTHER COUNTRY.
THE TOWER BLACKPOOL. 1915.
PHOTO: J.P. HAMBER BLACKPOOL.

Pauline Rivers and the ballet entered a new phase under the direction of Annette Schultz, known to millions simply as "Annette". One of her pupils was Elizabeth Larner, later to become a famous concert singer, starring in many London musicals and taking over the lead in *Kiss me Kate* at a minute's notice. When Annette died in 1953 the direction of the company passed to Joan Davis, who already had more than eighty shows to her credit and in 1951 was producing four shows all running concurrently in London. Although her name featured on the programmes as the producer, the day-to-day work was in the main undertaken by a Blackpool-based ballet mistress and choreographer, and for many years this day-to-day operation was in the capable hands of Mary Cregan, herself a past member of the ballet.

Auditions were held in the circus ring some

The programme of the jubilee production of the Children's Ballet in the nineteen-thirties.

BERTINI and the FAMOUS TOWER BROADCAST BAND
REGINALD DIXON at the NEW WONDER WURLITZER
M.C.—H. G. ROSCOE.

IN THE BALLROOM.   NIGHTLY AT 7-0.   SATURDAYS AT 3-15 and 7-0.
JUBILEE PRODUCTION of the Grand Spectacular CHILDREN'S BALLET:

"SILVER BELLS"

Devised and Produced by
Madame PAULINE RIVERS.
Assisted by LITTLE EMMIE.

1. Opening Ensemble. "Singing a Happy Song: JOAN ROE and Tiny Tots.
2. "Pop goes your Heart": BETTY McALLISTER, the Tower Girls.
3. "Easter Parade": JESSIE HANSON, KATHLEEN McALLISTER.
4. "Pop-eye, the Sailor Man": LITTLE VIOLET, MARY EASTON, and the Tower Girls.
5. "When I grow too old to Dream": Sung by LITTLE EDIE and IRENE.
6. "Dancing in a Dream": MARY CHANDLER. JOAN STOCK. and VERA JOHNSON.
7. "Keep Tempo": McALLISTER SISTERS.
8. Silly Symphony Parade.
9. "Congratulate Me": Sung by BETTY McALLISTER.
10. Acrobatic Dance: "Everything is Hunky Dooley."
11. Hawaiian Serenade, "Malola": Sung by LILY HILL.
12. Sylvia Ballet. Premiere Danseuse: KATHLEEN McALLISTER.
13. "Home Again": Tap Dance by MARY CHANDLER.
14. "Song of the Little Toy Drum": Chorus of Toy Soldiers— NORMA MEREDITH.
15. Finale: "Gentleman, the King."

Mde. PAULINE RIVERS.

weeks before the season started; the queue of children, mainly girls, would stretch all round the Tower and along the Promenade. Out of the hundreds of hopeful applicants about 150 would be chosen. They had to be at least twelve years old; rules regarding schooling and behaviour were rigorously applied, and closely monitored by education officers and watchful matrons. If the children missed school they were not allowed to attend rehearsals or performances; makeup was limited and sparingly applied to achieve an effect of naturalness, and such exotic additions as eye makeup were strictly forbidden. After the show they had to go straight home, having first removed all traces of the makeup under the scrutiny of the matrons. And in no circumstances were they allowed to talk to any members of the Tower staff, even members of the orchestra. In termtime there were evening performances only, but during the summer holidays there were afternoon shows as well. Although the girls were paid they never received more than a nominal sum, reaching little more than a pound a week in the nineteen-fifties, with a few shillings more for the principals.

There was no special charge for the public to see the ballet. The Tower admission fee of a shilling (rising to 1s 9d by the end of the nineteen-forties) entitled the visitor to go into the Aquarium, the Menagerie and floral gardens, to listen to an organ concert in the ballroom and to dance to the Tower orchestra, and also to watch the children's performance; it was excellent value by any standards. Many families came to the Tower specially to see the performance of the Children's Ballet, and half an hour before the show was due to start children would be lining the ballroom floor in eager anticipation.

There have always been plenty of amusements in the Tower for children apart from the Menagerie and Aquarium. For many years there was a puppet theatre run by Cambria Puppets on the stage in the Roof Gardens, and also in the Roof Gardens was a Punch and Judy show presented by Professor Moore. Both these attractions finished shortly after the Second World War.

The Children's Ballet, too, was brought to an untimely end in the seventies as a result of legislation which limited the number of days in

The finale of a Children's Ballet performance in the nineteen-fifties. With a cast of considerably more than a hundred, these were spectacular shows, yet there was no extra entrance fee to be paid by visitors to see them; the Tower admission fee entitled the visitor to see the Children's Ballet as well as to enjoy the Tower's other facilities.

Left: *A lively performance by the Children's Ballet in the nineteen-fifties.*

Below left: *A poster advertising "Blackpool Tower Children's Spectacular 1949 Ballet", featuring 120 children and produced by Annette Schultz.*

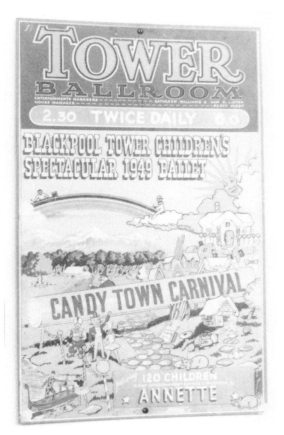

a year on which children might work to considerably fewer than the season required.

A Christmas attraction for local children was the mammoth Christmas tree installed each December in the ballroom. The tree, from the Lake District, was 50 feet high; to enable it to be brought into the ballroom it had to be cut in half, the two halves being dowelled together after the base had been planted in a 36-gallon beer-barrel. With scaffolding around the tree and the branches ingeniously supported, the electricians were able to start at the top to festoon the tree with coloured lights, dropping each row of branches as they worked their way down to the base of the tree; finally the tree was sprayed with fireproofing solution and then decorated with three thousand gaily wrapped presents.

When the day arrived for the presents to be distributed children had to pay a shilling admission, receiving in return a ticket bearing a number 1, 2, 3 or 4, entitling them to a gift from a particular area of the tree. The quarters numbered one to three contained fairly modest presents, but the fourth quarter bore more expensive and desirable gifts.

While it was supposed to be a matter of chance which number ticket a child received there is little doubt that a certain amount of selection was involved as families of staff or friends arrived at the ticket office. Nevertheless, every child appeared to be happily satisfied, and the scene in the ballroom soon resembled a giant party which had gone somewhat awry, with attendants viewing the scene ruefully.

Father Christmas was in attendance for those wishing to order their presents in advance. He must often have hoped that in some miraculous way their parents would see that the desired toys arrived on the due date.

One year the man doing duty as Father Christmas found the Tower Sergeant, who also happened to be the staff timekeeper, standing in the line of children queuing to speak to the red-coated figure. When the sergeant reached the head of the line Father Christmas jovially asked him, "And what would you like, my good man?" "What I want is your b—— time sheet", the sergeant growled, and for the next half-hour the children had to wait while Father Christmas filled in his time sheet.

It was repeatedly pointed out to Douglas Bickerstaffe that neither the huge Christmas tree with its load of presents nor the Father Christmas service was a paying proposition, but Douglas said it was his way of thanking local people for their support over the year. The goodwill effect was undoubtedly greater than the cost to the Tower Company, so the service remained.

But the Tower has to keep up with changing styles. Not for today's children are the static pleasures of sitting and watching other children sing and dance, nor do they want to watch puppets or Punch and Judy shows. For today's sophisticated children the sedate floral gardens, retaining many of their exotic plants and the gigantic grape clusters, have been converted to a tarzan-like setting appropriately named "Jungle Jim's". Every type of activity and variation of assault course, guaranteed to tire the most energetic child, can be found here. For very small active children there is a "soft play" area where, in complete safety, youngsters can jump, bounce, slide and roll to their hearts' content, while thankful parents can sit and watch.

There is a "Haunted Dungeon" for those who revel in blood-curdling thrills, and for the child (or parent) with a scientific bent "Out of this world" contains every variety of space-age marvel and optical illusion. The perennially popular Aquarium remains, fascinating children and adults alike.

Today the Tower probably offers under one roof a greater variety of attractions for all ages than any amusement park or palace in the country.

The changing face of children's entertainment: boisterous youngsters enjoying the delights of "Jungle Jim's".

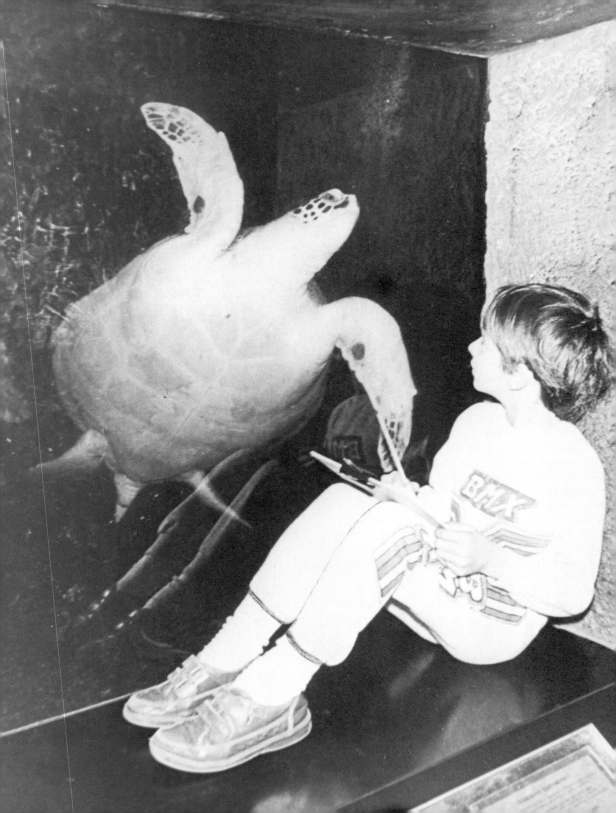

The Menagerie and the Aquarium 11

WHEN Dr Cocker opened his Menagerie, Aquarium and Aviary in 1874 they were an instant success with the Victorian public mainly as a curiosity, for fish, tropical birds and wild animals were relatively unknown to the Lancashire mill workers. While the public's primary interest was not in the welfare of the animals and birds, which were displayed in small confining cages, conservation and animal welfare did become a matter of importance to the Tower Company after the First World War, and today the Aquarium (which alone survives) maintains an important conservation and breeding programme for many endangered and rare species.

With the construction of the Tower the Menagerie, Aviary and Aquarium were incorporated into the Tower buildings, and when the Tower was completed the Aquarium remained on the ground floor, the Menagerie and Monkey House moved up to the second floor, and the Aviary was located on the third floor. It was a boast of the Menagerie that an animal there lived longer than the average life span of its species and the mortality rate in the Tower Menagerie was said to be the lowest in the country; many healthy litters were bred each year.

One of the most popular features, of course, was the daily chimpanzees' tea party at which anything could—and did—happen. Spectators at the front of the crowd were in danger of being drenched in lukewarm stickily sweet tea, to the delight of the apes and other onlookers.

As the company considered that bears needed open air a bear pit was located on the roof. It was overlooked by visitors enjoying tea in the outdoor cafe adjoining the roof gardens; no doubt the bears benefited greatly from table titbits and enjoyed the spectacle of humans eating just as much as the humans enjoyed watching the antics of the bears.

In the Aviary many colourful birds were kept in cages containing tropical pools. An experiment after the Second World War of

turning this into a free-flight area, with nets to prevent the birds crashing into the glass roof or getting out of doors, was not a complete success as the birds managed to get under the nets into impossible places. A great deal of time was spent in locating and rescuing them.

Another experiment with the animals resulted in even greater chaos. Cages with wires instead of bars were installed giving visitors a better view of the animals with, it was thought, complete safety. While the curator and attendants could not move the tightly strung wires, which were no thicker than piano wires, the wires proved to be no obstacle to the bears, who parted them easily and simply walked out—bringing that experiment to a rapid conclusion.

Changing patterns in animal care brought a proposal from the Tower Company to Blackpool Corporation in 1970 that an open-air zoo

A contemporary artist's impression of the Aquarium, 1925.

be started. A year later Blackpool Zoo was formally opened at the back of Stanley Park, thus determining the fate of the once-popular Menagerie; the Aviary had closed some time earlier.

The popularity of the Aquarium has never waned and it now ranks among the world's top aquaria. While it is still substantially the same as in Dr Cocker's time, alterations and additions over the years have imperceptibly altered it. Dr Cocker's original tanks were reconstructed and some were replaced a few years ago as water pressure and temperature expansion took their toll of the old slate beds; and the old vulcanite piping has been replaced. During these alterations one section of the salt-water tanks was propped up from the basement, allowing the removal of an old pillar standing in the salt-water tank below which had corroded away. A new steel stanchion was put in its place and covered with reinforced concrete for protection, the whole operation being carried out without causing the slightest

movement of the existing salt-water tanks. The original Aquarium tanks were supported on old flitch beams made from slices of huge pitchpine baulks with half-inch steel stiffening plates, the whole bolted together. These beams still survive.

Fish, like human beings, do not like rapid changes of temperature if they are to remain healthy. Constant supplies of fresh air must be introduced into the water for the fish to absorb and the water itself must be constantly changed. As seawater round the coast tends to be polluted it has to be rigorously cleaned in the treatment rooms, which contain pumps, filters, aerators, heaters, refrigerators and set-tling tanks.

The Aquarium has its own hatcheries and stocks are also supplied from British waters and from rivers and seas all over the world. The approximate quantities of salt and fresh water in the tanks is 35,000 gallons each. Both fresh and salt-water tanks are maintained, and there is a section of warm tropical tanks for exhibiting fish from warmer climates. For the interested aquarist further technical details are printed in the appendix.

The Tower's chief aquarist, Mr Harry Willacy, one of the top five aquarists in the country, is proud of the fact that his fish live longer, grow to greater size, and breed better than many fish in their own habitat. In their tanks they are free from predators and natural hazards. In many cases preservation of rare and endangered species is helped considerably by concerned aquaria such as the Tower Aquarium.

Like the lift, the Aquarium is a very expen-sive item in the Tower's budget, but it would be unthinkable for it not to be there, playing its own part in conservation and education.

Attendants still receive inquiries from visi-tors about the famed Orchestrion, which was such a popular feature for nearly a century. As old as the Aquarium itself, the Orchestrion was installed by Dr Cocker at the entrance so that its music could be heard on the Promenade, thus attracting visitors into the building.

Working on the principle of a large barrel

The Orchestrion which was used by Dr Cocker to attract visitors into the Aquarium.

organ, it was in its day considered a musical marvel. People crowded round it to listen; for many it was their first introduction to classical music. Originally it was operated by weights, much as a grandfather clock, but before the First World War it was equipped with an electric motor. At the same time the huge spiked barrels which played the tunes were replaced with paper rolls. It was cleaned and overhauled in 1949; the only thing added at that time were new paper rolls, for the pre-vious ones had completely worn out.

Most of the people who today remember it believe that the organ was coin operated, but this was never so. The music was supplied free of charge.

Old age and changing tastes settled the fate of the organ, which went into honourable retirement. It is now proudly displayed in a Birmingham museum.

The elephants are always a popular part of the Circus performance, even if their contribution is sometimes a little unexpected.

The Circus   12

" A PALACE of Pleasure in itself" was the description given by John Bickerstaffe to the circus in his early programmes. One of the few permanent circuses in Britain, it has entertained audiences for nearly a hundred years, and will surely continue to do so into another century.

The first performance took place on Whit Monday, 14th May, 1894, and the circus has not missed a season since, playing to packed houses through two world wars and through the great depression of the nineteen-thirties. And in all those years it has never failed to thrill families, adults and children alike, with its spectacular and daring acts brought from all over the world.

A distinctive and valuable accessory of the Blackpool circus which at the time of its installation was unique is the sinking floor which made possible the staging of the always spectacular water finale. As Sir John put it in his programme, "A novel feature of the circus is that the floor of the arena can be lowered by hydraulic mechanism and converted within one minute into an aquatic area six feet deep being filled with thousands of gallons of water".

In the early days the circus was billed as an "Aquatic and variety circus", for the Tower Company were rightly proud of their ability to provide something that was quite beyond the capabilities of any travelling circus. The finale was described in the first programme as a "Most magnificent water pantomime entitled 'Undine, or the Water fairies ballet', terminating with a laughable farce".

For the said laughable conclusion the redoubtable Oliver Gaggs put on a false wig and provided his own comic act. And prudish Victorian ladies who might have wondered about the appearance of water fairies in public were assured that the swimmers were all fully costumed.

The water spectacle, magnificent as it undoubtedly is, always provides a fitting finale to the show. It takes less than two minutes for the circus ring to be transformed into a water fairyland, 40,000 gallons of water being pumped in to provide a pool large enough for swimming displays and impressively illuminated tableaux. After the Second World War the swimming displays were discontinued but the water spectacles, with imaginative and elaborately illuminated scenes, continued to provide a breathtaking end to an always superb circus performance. Then in 1987 the finale again included a swimming display, a welcome return to the old routine.

Although the circus was mainly a summer entertainment, there have in the past been many years when a special Christmas circus competed with pantomimes in the local theatres. For many years the season lasted thirty-two weeks, with performances each day at 11.15 am, 3 pm and 7.30 pm. Before the Second World War prices varied between sixpence and half a crown, and throughout the season more than 650 letters a day applying for advance bookings would be received at the box office; these were dealt with by a staff of fourteen booking clerks.

The tattered bill advertising "The Tower
Aquatic and Variety Circus", which included a
group of performing animals consisting of
lions, boarhounds and ponies.

Successive circus directors have scoured the
world for unusual and entertaining acts, and
many promising artists who have appeared in
the circus ring have gone on to find fame either
in other circuses or in different fields

altogether. Among the latter was a comic
juggler named W. C. Fields, who became a
legend in the cinema as one of the world's
funniest film actors.

Bernard Crabtree, a circus director for many
years after the Second World War, travelled
tirelessly to find new acts, drawing on his
extensive knowledge and experience to judge
which acts would be popular. As he says, "Not
every circus act appeals to English audiences,
however famous they are in their own country". He has brought many promising but
unknown artists to Blackpool who have gone
on to find fame in other circuses; it still is the
ambition of every circus artist to be seen in this
prestigious circus.

Ring masters, in their immaculate attire, are
always much admired. Before the Second
World War George Lockhart was perhaps the
most famous. A splendid figure in his shiny top
hat and red jacket, he carried a large whip
which was used only for effect, never on the
animals. His father, who had appeared in the
early days of the circus with a troupe of
elephants and lions, had been ring master
before him.

Most ring masters have at some time worked
in the circus as performers, so they are well
aware of the problems an artist may have to
face, particularly an artist whose English may
be limited to two or three words; with such
people a great deal of tact may be necessary.

Sometimes the few words an artist learns can
be slightly embarrassing or amusing when the
audience hears them. There was the man who
was taught to say "Ee, by gum, muck" when he
saw any droppings in the ring; when the
audience laughed he asked with the utmost
seriousness, "What does it mean?".

"Muck", of course, is inseparable from the
circus ring. One programme in quite recent
years contained a scene in which a space-age
rocket spouting flames from its rear appeared
through a sea of dry ice, with the clowns
dressed as Martians sweeping the floor with
geiger counters. In a rather loud voice one lady
in the audience asked in puzzlement, "What
are they looking for?", to be answered im-

Performing sealions have always been a popular circus act.

mediately by one of the Martians, "Looking for 'orse muck, Mum!"

The audience welcomes anything unrehearsed and accidental. One night a crowded audience watched fascinated as an eager young ring attendant who had been told to keep the ring clean during the animal acts, seeing an elephant decorate the ring with two large droppings, dashed immediately into the ring with a brush and shovel; he was bending down to sweep up the animal's offerings when the third and largest effort landed squarely on his head, reducing the audience to hysterics.

The tables were turned on the audience, however, when one evening a young attendant, attaching the water hose to the fountains for the water finale, made the connection incorrectly; when the water was switched on the hose immediately began to spray the ringside viewers. People in the seats behind thought this hugely amusing, until the connection broke loose and, waving about like an elephant's trunk, sprayed everyone liberally. Fortunately no real harm was done and the audience treated the whole thing as part of an enjoyable performance, clapping vigorously as one of the circus staff hastily put the connection right.

There can never be the slightest doubt that one of the main attractions of the circus is its animal acts. One can only respect and support the views of concerned animal rights activists who protest against cases of extreme cruelty such as hare coursing, badger baiting, dog fighting and inhumanity to domestic pets, but one has less sympathy for demands that animal acts be banned from the circus. Cruelty in circuses is rare in the extreme, and it would be sad indeed if the happy relationship between animals and their trainers were to become a thing of the past.

The animals themselves can be very individualistic and are quite capable of making up their own minds, sometimes to the discomfort of their human partners. An elephant once decided to carry out his own investigations backstage and, despite the entreaties of his handler, made an unannounced entrance into the ring through a curtained doorway that was too small for his bulk. He strolled uncon-

Some of the lavish decoration in the Circus, which has a quite different atmosphere from that of the traditional Big Top.

accident in the ring; he could not bring himself to leave the circus, staying on instead to help the clowns—and doing it so well that he became the most famous clown of his day.

"Doodles", as he was called, was a tiny figure only 4 feet 10 inches tall, taking size 1½ in shoes, and with his own unusual brand of humour—no one ever quite discovered how he managed to chase his hat round the ring, but it had the audiences rolling in the aisles. In time he became internationally famous, but even Doodles' bright star was eclipsed by the man who eventually replaced him, the unique and lovable Charlie Cairoli.

Born in Italy, Charlie came from a family with a long circus tradition; his real name was Carletto. With his father and brother he formed part of the "Trio Cairoli", working in circuses all over the world. While in Paris he fell in love with the beautiful Violette, a talented acrobat from another circus family. They married in Paris in 1934, but had no honeymoon for some years as Charlie had to appear twice in the ring on the day of his wedding and each day for the following few weeks. The show definitely came first with the Cairoli family, as it does with all circus performers.

Like Doodles, Charlie did not start as a clown. He was an accomplished musician, but his sense of fun and his irrepressible humour never allowed him to be serious for long, and it was a natural step for him to adjust his act to that of a clown, at which he became a master. His clown mask was simple; as he said, "You must never frighten children", and he put on only a cherry-red nose which, with his naturally sparkling eyes, gave him a wickedly mischievous look. Although children adored him he insisted he was not just a children's entertainer; he worked as much to the adult audience, captivating them with his endearing and timeless antics. Well aware that even slapstick must be updated to suit an increasingly sophisticated audience, he ensured that his act was always in keeping with the trends of the day.

Charlie came to Blackpool in 1939 for the

cernedly into the ring gaily decked with the curtains from the doorway—and insisted on using the entrance for the rest of the season.

Then there was the lion that discovered one night that he could easily open the door of his cage. The following morning he was found by his owner, after a worried search, snoring peacefully in the warmth of the engine room not far away. When wakened he trotted back quite amiably to his cage to resume his sleep there.

Running a close second to the animal acts as the children's favourites must be the clowns. The first billed clowns to achieve fame were a couple known as August and September, who had a style of comedy all their own. On the same bill was an acrobat, William (Billy) Patrick McAllister, who had a rather bad

The audience take their seats for a performance in the Circus. One of the legs of the Tower can be seen in the middle of the picture, disguised by a wealth of decoration covered in gold leaf.

one season, but on the outbreak of the Second World War that September he was interned as an alien and sent to the Isle of Man, not being released until 1946. He became a British citizen shortly after his release.

When he and his wife first arrived in England neither of them spoke much English. During their first week in Blackpool Violette went to the butcher's; bewildered by the array of meat and with no knowledge of how to ask for what she wanted, she pointed to a tray of chops, held up two fingers and smiled at the butcher, who obligingly said, "Two chops? Yes, certainly, Madam" and wrapped them up. Violette returned home triumphantly to serve them for dinner. Next day she asked again for "Two chops", remembering what the butcher had said. Unable to ask for other cuts of meat, she continued each day to ask for "Two chops", until at the end of the week Charlie demanded in exasperation, "Don't they sell anything in England but b——— chops?".

In the circus Charlie worked with Paul, a white-faced clown who was also a brilliant musician, and Little Jimmy, the inevitable fall-guy for Charlie's tricks but one who in the

85

Above: *This programme of the Blackpool Tower Circus features Charlie Cairoli as one of the stars of the show.*

Opposite page: *Charlie Cairoli as everyone remembers him.*

Left: *Charlie Cairoli is presented to the Queen and the Duke of Edinburgh after a Royal Command Performance.*

nd usually managed to turn the tables on everybody, to the delight of the audience. For ome years Charlie's own son, Charlie Junior, orked with him in his act before leaving to orm his own act.

Master of the ad-lib, Charlie was never verse to involving the audience in some utrageous piece of business—an involvement hich, needless to say, the audience loved. uch was his appeal and so popular his act that was impossible for anyone to follow him; nly the spectacular water finale could bring the erformance to a close.

Behind the scenes Charlie had his own way f dealing with other circus performers who ied to take advantage of him. When he found at someone was helping himself to his hair eam, Charlie replaced it with a white rubber dhesive, which quickly revealed the culprit. nd when he realized that someone was elping himself to cigarettes from his dressing om, Charlie replaced them with a mild xplosive imitation cigarette.

Charlie was equally capable of dealing with e situation in reverse. When the present ell-known ring master Norman Barrett found necessary to remonstrate with Charlie over me minor misdemeanour he found it difficult keep a serious face, confronted by a solemn own with a large fly on his red nose.

Charlie was invited to Monte Carlo for a orld circus convention. Prince Rainier was osting the celebrated gathering and in honour the occasion a special issue of Monaco amps bearing Charlie's portrait was printed; harlie was very proud to return home with a mple sheet of the stamps. But perhaps his oudest moment came when he chatted with e Queen and the Duke of Edinburgh after ppearing in a Command Performance; not any clowns have appeared in Royal Com- and Performances.

Each season he received hundreds of fan tters from children and adults. When he died the age of seventy shortly after retiring on octor's orders, forty years after joining the ower circus, thousands of adults and children ied for "Uncle Charlie".

As yet no one has taken Charlie's place; possibly nobody ever will. The memory of Charlie playing *You are my heart's delight* on a muted trumpet to a wide-eyed child in the audience is one that will remain in the hearts of thousands of people who were captivated by the magic of Charlie Cairoli.

One year a party of Russian diplomats visited the circus. They were amazed not only by the high standard of the performance but also by the outstanding beauty of their sur- roundings. And well they might, for the setting between the four legs of the Tower provides a breathtaking sight for those who look around them, with the gilded walls and ceiling and the massive girders encasing the whole arena.

In the centre of the ring is the place where the first post was sunk into the ground for the positioning of the four legs. If the ceiling were transparent one would be able to look straight up to the top of the Tower.

The Russians were even more astonished to

discover that the show was not one reserved for distinguished guests, but that the general public were allowed in to see it whenever they wished.

The circus ring has been used over the years for many entertainments apart from the circus itself. Among the winter attractions in the arena is boxing, possibly starting in 1919 with a boxing display given by champion Jimmy Wilde; there were regular programmes of both boxing and wrestling in later years. One of the most popular—and most hated—wrestlers was Jack Pye, who to the boos and hisses of the audience indulged in every foul and dirty trick in the book; but out of the ring he was polite and charming. For a number of winters Joe Davis and Walter Lindrum gave billiard demonstrations—and were paid £2 10s (£2.50) for each performance.

Occasionally the circus was billed as a playhouse, and one year there was even a performance of Shakespeare in the round. During the Second World War and in the early post-war years there were Sunday concerts of both classical and modern music. One concert

Above left: *One of the imposing entrances to the Circus, with decoration reminiscent of some Eastern potentate's palace.*

Right: *Blackpool Brownies meet the clowns.*

Left: *Looking down on the Circus ring from high up in the gallery; here one is easily aware of the Tower's legs and the steel arch linking them.*

featuring Cleo Laine and her trio was given to a full house.

The thorny question of whether or not animals should be employed to entertain an audience will not be easily resolved, but one can say that there is no cruelty involved in training animals for a circus. The animals are too valuable to abuse, and a performance by a cowed animal would be instantly detected by the audience. There is no doubt that the animals appearing at the Tower Circus have always been well looked after.

In 1930 the Tower Company bought land at Staining which included a brewery known as the Queens Brewery. This building was used as a bottling plant for the bar supplies and the land was converted to winter quarters for the circus animals. Stables were erected and exercise grounds and a circus ring were laid out.

When the workshops were closed thirty years later the Staining grounds were sold, and today most of the circus animals spend the winter with other circuses; some go abroad. This part of the operation is now run by an independent company.

It would certainly be sad if the mix of animals and human performers were to be broken up because of the belief that animal training must perforce involve some degree of cruelty or degradation. We would all be a little poorer for the loss of this particular form of family entertainment.

Maintenance

13

THE THOUSANDS of visitors who pay for admission to the Tower every day spare very little thought for those who work so hard to ensure the success of their visit.

A very large back-up service is needed to ensure that the Tower complex runs smoothly, that the lifts continue operating efficiently, that the dining rooms and bars receive supplies, that air continues to be pumped into the tanks in the Aquarium, and that there are no breakdowns which will interrupt visitors' enjoyment.

At one time the back-up team consisted of nearly a hundred and fifty men, including the "stick-men", the experts with the special knowledge and skill to care for the largest steel tower in the country and its handmaiden, the lift system. They get their name from the affectionate nickname given to the Tower itself, which to generations of Tower Company employees has been "the stick".

The staff also includes engineers, electricians, fitters, joiners, plumbers, riveters, riggers and a host of other skilled and semi-skilled tradesmen. All have an essential part to play in maintaining the Tower and its buildings, along with an elaborate air filter system, a large underfloor tank for flooding the circus ring—one of only three in the world—a cellar system for supplying the numerous bars, amusement machines to rival any amusement arcade in Blackpool, and much else besides.

For over eighty years the Tower Company had its own fully-equipped workshops, even a blacksmith's forge, but for economic reasons the workshops have closed in recent years and much of the work is now contracted out.

There is still a sizeable corps of maintenance men engaged all the year round on overhauling, checking and repairing the Tower and the contents of its buildings. Much of the work has to be done at night or during the winter.

The stick-men have to deal with an enemy which wages constant war on the steelwork of the Tower. It is a factor which those responsible for maintaining the Eiffel Tower do not have to take into account. The enemy is salt, borne in abundance on the westerly winds which sweep in from the Irish Sea.

On a windy day salt deposits can be found even 300 feet up the Tower. The corrosive properties of the salt spray are such that a protective coat of paint has to be constantly replaced. It takes seven years to paint the Tower from top to bottom, and as soon as one

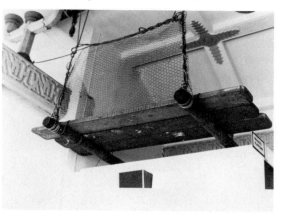

Left: *When painting the steelwork of the Tower it is a matter of "one hand for the ship and one for yourself".*

Below left: *One of the "stick-men", Bernard Howard, engaged on maintenance work on the Tower.*

coat has been completed the application of the next has to begin.

Work on the outside of the structure is not without its risks, and although many precautions are taken accidents have occurred to the stick-men. In the nineteen-sixties one of the stick-men, forty-two-year-old Joe Thomas, fell to his death when a pole holding the platform on which he was working broke. His companion on the platform, Richard Entwistle, managed to hold on to the girderwork of the Tower with one hand while clutching two planks of the broken platform with the other in an attempt to hold it up. He maintained his hold until fellow-workers arrived to rescue him.

For the first forty years of its existence the Tower was painted with purple oxide, and then in 1935 a switch was made to red oxide. Each coat consists of nine tons of red lead and a ton and a half of red oxide. As a result of the accumulation of coat upon coat the paint is in places as much as half an inch thick. Despite the use of red oxide, the Tower does not appear red, for the salt-laden air turns the paint black almost immediately it is applied.

Some wit once suggested that luminous paint might be used so that the Tower would glow at night, but the idea was turned down by the

Bernard Howard working on one of the pinnacles at the top of the Tower.

Tower Company. Not that the company is totally against changing the look of the Tower; for the Queen's Silver Jubilee in 1977 it was given a coat of silver paint, and for that summer the Tower shone in the sunshine, playing its own part in the celebrations.

On a later royal occasion the Tower was decked with flags to mark the wedding of Prince Charles and Lady Diana Spencer—and from the flagpole at the top of the Tower floated a nine-foot flag such as used to be flown every day in Sir John's time. Such a flag could be completely shredded in the course of one gusty day, and the high cost of large flags now restricts their use to special occasions.

Each year the Tower becomes an integral part of the famous Blackpool Illuminations, which for more than a hundred years have provided an annual attraction to the town, except, of course, during the war years. The Tower was first illuminated in the autumn of 1925, when it bore in coloured lights the modest legend bestowed on the building by Sir John, "Wonderland of the world". The work of

93

decorating the Tower is carried out by the company's own electricians and maintenance staff; the job takes two to three months and involves the use of more than 10,000 bulbs.

Apart from the four huge feet in their concrete blocks, much of the outside metal-work of the structure has been replaced as corrosion takes its effect. Of the original parts still left, the main plates and, below roof level,

Lit by more than 10,000 bulbs, the Tower forms an integral part of the town's Illuminations.

the four huge struts which run to the base of the building are as good as the day they were installed. The Tower above roof level, however, has virtually all been replaced. Thirty-five feet from the top is the newest piece of all: the top was removed during the war and had to be replaced when peace returned.

The lifts are an important and integral part of the service the Tower Company must offer. And a service it undoubtedly is, for the lifts have been running at a loss for many years. When the Tower first opened the charge for the ascent was a shilling, but this was quickly reduced to sixpence, at which level it remained until well after the First World War, when it reverted to a shilling. Eventually it became clear that the charge bore no relation to the installation and maintenance costs of the lifts, which were far from being a paying proposition. Yet it was unthinkable for the lifts not to run; what use is a 500-foot Tower if you cannot go to the top and see the finest view in the North of England? Shrugging their shoulders philosophically, the directors decided that rather than increase the lift charge they would include the lifts as part of the Tower service, with the general admission price including the ride to the top of the Tower.

Today the lifts make 50,000 trips a year, covering over 3,000 miles, each journey taking approximately two minutes. The original hydraulic lifts were very noisy because of the types of runners at the sides of the cars. Between 1952 and 1957 a new electric lift system was installed by Babcock Robey, of Lincoln, a prominent firm of mining lift suppliers and fitters, working in conjunction with the Otis Elevator Company, and the lifts now run so silently that a warning bell has to be fitted to alert the painters or riggers to the car's approach. The electric lifts are controlled from a huge engine room, which from its appearance could be the engine room of a modern liner.

When the equipment was installed the proximity of nearby buildings prevented the massive machinery being lifted by crane up to the 85-foot level where it is housed. It had to be dismantled and carried through the building piece by piece, entailing a lot of manual effort and much colourful language. (Full details of both the hydraulic and electric lift systems are given in the appendix.)

Security at the Tower top is an ever-present problem. Prominent notices warn of the penalties for throwing objects from the top, and a series of TV observation cameras constantly record the behaviour of people at the Tower top. Such precautions help to deter the few irresponsible people who behave thoughtlessly, but to thwart of those who persist in throwing things blue netting has been stretched around the superstructure; regrettable though the presence of the netting might be, it is reasonably unobtrusive.

One tricky job for the maintenance men each spring is to lower the large gold chandeliers in the ballroom for cleaning. This nerve-wracking task takes several days, and is done under the supervision of Reg Campbell. The bulbs and glasswork are painstakingly washed and the intricate gold work polished by hand until it recovers its glitter and sparkle, human breath and smoke having dulled all the metalwork in the course of the season.

A cheerful group of "stick-men" at work high above the Blackpool seafront.

In 1961 the company gave the Tower buildings a facelift, replacing and renovating much of the frontage and removing the pinnacles and turrets which had become unsafe. The whole exercise cost more than it had cost to build the Tower in 1894. Now listed as a building of historic or architectural interest, the Tower is lovingly maintained and there is an ongoing programme of rescuing and restoring the many beautiful terracotta panels and the stained glass windows in the Tower buildings. In 1984 the present company spent over two million pounds on redecorating, restoring and updating the various lounges and halls and on giving attention to the structure of the building.

Maintenance of the Tower and buildings is under the direction of the Unit Engineer, Mr Eric Redfern, successor to Mr George Foster. Mr Redfern knows intimately every inch of his Tower.

He was delighted when in December, 1984, he was invited with a colleague to visit the Eiffel Tower in Paris. It was a goodwill visit with much friendliness on both sides as well as, no doubt, a great deal of professional curiosity. Mr Redfern was intrigued to discover that in Paris they still have the original hydraulic lift system, as efforts to modernise the system had been thwarted by preservation orders.

As the water in the pumps and tanks freezes in the Parisian winter the hydraulic lift service is suspended from November to March, an electric lift being used instead. Blackpool's lift was placed in the basement of the buildings and the engine room was heated, thus helping to prevent this problem arising; the addition of glycerine as an anti-freeze, which does not appear to be used in Paris, also aids the prevention of freezing. As the Parisian air does not contain a great deal of salt the Eiffel Tower rarely needs repainting and corrosion is less of a problem than at Blackpool, although petrol pollution during the past few years from traffic

Engineer George Foster looking at part of the hydraulic lift machinery in the north-east leg of the Tower.

Above: *The hoist room, with the winding drums for the two lifts on the left.*

Left: *Mr Reg Campbell checking the draught beer in the stores beneath the Tower's bars.*

passing between the legs has led to the base of one of the legs having to be replaced. Like the New Brighton tower, the Eiffel Tower is much lacier in appearance than that at Blackpool, and the ease of maintenance is, therefore, fortunate or like its Cheshire counterpart it might not have survived the years.

The Ballroom Fire 14

DISASTER came unexpectedly in the early morning of 14th December, 1956, when fire broke out in the ballroom. It was probably caused by a cigarette dropped in a chair in an office near the crushroom separating the ballroom from the buffet room.

It was at 6.50 am that Mr Sam Soutter, making his routine inspection of the building, saw smoke coming from a window in Bank Hey Street. The fire had probably been smouldering away all night.

By the time twenty-five firemen with four engines and a turntable ladder arrived the flames had a thorough hold. Fire officers took one look and called in other firemen with their engines from Fleetwood and St Annes.

The firemen were dismayed at the terrible sight confronting them as flames belched out of windows which exploded in the heat.

For hours staff and firemen worked side by side to save the building. Two of the firemen were overcome by fumes in the smoke-filled building and two members of the Tower staff, Mr Soutter and Mr G. Platt, also had to be taken to hospital for treatment. So many thousands of gallons of water were poured into the burning building that it cascaded down the stairs and escaped under the entrance doors on to the promenade.

Zoo curator Mr Legge was soon on the scene and throughout the firefighting operations remained with his animals in the Menagerie, calming them and managing to ensure their safety. In the Aviary the birds were less fortunate; many were overcome by the smoke which filled the entire building and twenty-one died, including a particularly valuable parrot.

By lunchtime, after five hours of desperate firefighting, it was thought the flames had been brought under control. But still smoke billowed out from the ballroom floor, and investigations revealed that the fire was anything but out; it was very much alive, and spreading under the dance floor.

Firemen began hacking at the wooden blocks in an effort to reach the underfloor fire, helped in their work by the spotlights which on happier occasions had been used to illuminate dancing couples. Douglas Bickerstaffe, then chairman of the Tower Company, watched helplessly as the firemen tore up the magnificent dance floor and he shed tears as he realised the damage the fire was causing.

The staff rescued as much as they could, including thousands of pounds' worth of musical instruments belonging to Charles Barlow's Tower band. The bandsmen themselves worked frantically to save their sheet music, Charles Barlow himself throwing the sheets through an open window to his men in the street below.

As the smoke gradually cleared the destruction caused by the inferno was revealed. "It's like a scene out of hell" said one fireman. With the fire out at last dismayed staff viewed the great holes in the floor and the damaged decorations hanging in blackened clusters; burnt debris lay all over the place.

It had been fortunate, said the fire chief, that a strong southerly wind had kept the flames

Left: *Fire damage to the Wurlitzer organ, which was fortunately by no means as serious as might have been expected.*

Right: *Water from the firemen's hoses adds to the desolation in the cafe after the fire.*

Below left: *Workmen begin clearing the ballroom floor, torn up by firemen trying to reach the seat of the fire.*

from the centre of the building, which escaped with little more than smoke damage. And later the investigating team trying to ascertain the cause of the fire declared that it had been fortunate that when the Tower was built the orchestra platform had been put on a concrete base which stretched halfway down the side of the ballroom; this prevented the spread of the fire in that direction and saved the Wurlitzer from worse damage than it sustained. The foresight of the original builders in encasing the legs in solid blocks of concrete ensured that there was little risk to the foundations of the building and to the Tower itself.

The ballroom was clearly going to be out of action for a long time, but the show must go on; the Palace ballroom, which had been closed for the winter, was reopened and for Charles Barlow and his band it was business as usual the following night. They played hastily-cleaned and renovated instruments but in their ordinary clothes, because their uniforms had been lost in the fire.

It took Mr McGinty and his staff seven weeks of hard work to clear up the mess before the massive job of restoration could be started. "It's a disaster of huge proportions", said Douglas Bickerstaffe as he contemplated the

enormity of the task before him. He realised the phenomenally high cost which would be involved, and he could have been forgiven if he had wondered if it was all going to be worth while.

But he had been hewn out of the same granite as his father, Alderman Tom, and his determined uncle, Sir John Bickerstaffe, and there was really no doubt in his mind about the course of action to be taken. Despite pressure to modernise the ballroom, he was firm in his decision that it should be restored in its original style as Frank Matcham had designed it. No matter that most of the craftsmen had gone and that some of the arts had been forgotten; no effort must be spared to find workmen who could gild, sculpt, plaster, paint and decorate exactly as they had done sixty years previously.

The architect of the new ballroom was Charles McKeith, and seventy-year-old Andrew Mazzei, whose father had worked on the ballroom so many years before, was brought out of retirement to serve as art director. Mr Mazzei, who had been a famous art director for the film industry, set to work to engage skilled workmen from far and near to carry out the work. Mr Peter Miller, the famous artist, was engaged to replace the ballroom murals, Mr James Bell designed a new lounge where the old Victoria Lounge had been and Mr Claude Harrison worked on artistic features in the new lounge.

Defective steelwork had first to be removed and replaced with a hundred tons of steel connected to the sound members of the structure. Soon the ballroom looked like a huge Meccano nightmare as scaffolding weighing forty tons and containing 107,000 feet of tubing was erected.

The sub-floor was reconstructed of concrete and steel, and over this were laid the springs and parquet flooring which formed the dance floor itself. For the carpeted areas cork lino was used as an underbase for the 3,000 square yards of specially woven carpet; laying it required twenty barrels of adhesive and a hundredweight of tacks. It took three months to lay and polish the dance floor itself, with a team of experts using 30,602 blocks of mahogany, oak and walnut; they used three hundredweight of nails and eight hundredweight of glue. Not only were the parquet blocks carefully sprung but an elaborate mechanism was installed which enabled the springs to be locked when seats were installed for conferences and stage performances.

The Wurlitzer organ was sent away to be completely overhauled and reconditioned, and while it was away a new organ pit was built allowing the organ console to be raised and lowered as required, leaving the stage clear when the organ was not in use. And, needless to say, a completely up-to-date sprinkler system was installed.

The final job was the restoration of the artwork, and for this Mr Mazzei and his team of craftsmen used 170 tons of plaster containing a fireproofer, with 68,000 yards of scrim, 600 gallons of paint, nearly 10,000 square feet of gold leaf, and 1,000 yards of metallic wallpaper imported from Switzerland.

In all, the work cost over half a million pounds and lasted eighteen months. When the ballroom was ready for reopening Douglas Bickerstaffe was asked which notable personality would perform the ceremony; many famous names were put forward. He turned them all down, saying that as ordinary folk had made the Tower and patronised the ballroom for nearly sixty years they would be the openers. Everyone who had attended the opening of the Tower and the ballroom in 1894 was invited; those who wrote in were sent tickets for the reopening dinner and celebration on 28th May, 1958.

Tower staff were included in the festivities, which began at 10.30 am on the opening day when the Tower buildings were thrown open to invited guests. Members of the staff joined VIPs in partaking of the drinks and refresh-

An advertisement of the re-opening of the Tower ballroom and lounge after its restoration following the 1956 fire.

ments, and at 11.30 there was a reception at the Bank Hey Street entrance for the invited guests, most of whom were at least in their seventies; many were even older. Those who wished to see the restored building were taken on a conducted tour before lunch, which was provided by the Tower Company, and afterwards they were entertained in the Oriental Lounge.

For the opening ceremony a special cake had been made in the form of a thirty-inch-high model of the Tower. The doors opened to the public at 6.30 pm, and an hour later Douglas Bickerstaffe took a knife and cut the cake.

There was dancing until midnight, with the elderly guests enjoying the lavishly colourful spectacle of the glittering new ballroom, even if their tired legs did not allow them to join in the dancing.

One of the guests was a Miss Lister, who proudly claimed that she and a friend had been the first persons on the floor of the Grand Pavilion when it opened; more recently she had been living in Florida. She remembered that the orchestra had been conducted by Oliver Gaggs. Two ladies whose father had leased the Temperance bar for three years also remembered dancing on the ballroom's first night.

Perhaps, watching the dancers in the new ballroom, Douglas might have felt, as Sir John had done over sixty years earlier, that after all the troubles the Tower had endured this particular story had had a happy ending.

A newspaper cutting recording the re-opening of the ballroom and featuring a picture of the cake cut by Douglas Bickerstaffe at the reopening ceremony.

'The Tower needs people' 15

THE BICKERSTAFFES were always well aware that the strength of the company lay not only in their own hands but also in the quality of the staff they employed; and they were ready to admit that they were backed by an excellent team of workers with the same dedication as themselves. As Douglas once said, "The people need the Tower, and the Tower needs people".

Between the wars a number of page boys were employed each year. After being fitted with a Tower uniform (which they wore with great pride), they were put under the direction and supervision of a stern-faced sergeant. Many of the page boys went on to become attendants, and many others entered various trades as vacancies occurred in the different departments. With 350 permanent staff, rising to 700 in the season, there were always plenty of opportunities for a keen boy or girl, and every encouragement was given by the company for employees to study and become qualified in a trade or profession.

Albert Hamilton started as a page boy, was able in due time to transfer as an apprentice to the plumbing department and rose to become one of the company's senior plumbers. Mr Hamilton recalls his first day as a page boy and the advice given to him by an older colleague that he should familiarise himself with the number of buttons on his uniform. "Why?" asked the new boy in surprise. He was informed that it was one of the commonest questions visitors would ask him as they viewed the impressive uniform with its array of brass buttons. If he could answer the question smartly (there were forty-four buttons) he would invariably get a tip; and by the end of the week tips could amount to a respectable sum.

Mr William McGinty remembers his days as a page boy, too. He started in the Tower-owned Grand Theatre and proudly wore a pillbox hat—the Tower page boys had a forage cap. Each evening during the stage performances he would sit in the booking office poring over his books, studying for exams which would give him the qualifications he wanted. He became the youngest theatre manager in the country when he was made manager of the Grand Theatre in 1937 at the age of twenty-one. After some narrow escapes from death during the war he returned to the Tower Company and was eventually made house manager of the Tower, holding that position until 1962.

A compassionate man, Mr McGinty rarely refused a request from an orphanage or poor children's home for special consideration for circus seats, fitting the party in at reduced rates on quiet matinees (there was a matinee performance of the circus every afternoon) on the principle that not only was it a special treat for the children but it helped swell the audience and thus enhance the circus atmosphere. This far-sighted gesture has since repaid the Tower handsomely; remembering happy visits as poor children or orphans, many people now bring parties of children or adults to the Tower and the circus.

It was the ambition of many of the page boys to become a Tower attendant and eventually a lofty sergeant, who supervised his own team of staff. The stately sergeants were respected by staff and visitors alike, and ruled both with awesome authority. Rarely were the police required to deal with Saturday night rowdies; a team of burly attendants was usually more than capable of dealing with any troublemakers.

Always ready to cope with an emergency, the sergeants were occasionally called upon to perform unusual tasks. One sergeant who had spent his childhood on a farm had no difficulty in delivering a kid, born to one of the goats in the children's farm, winning the applause as well as the admiration of watching staff.

Dealing with a lost child, convinced that his parents had abandoned him for ever, was just an everyday task. One small child sobbed to sergeant who displayed an unexpectedly gentle side as he cradled the lost youngster, "I've los me Mam, and I was enjoying meself".

Many of the staff became deeply involved in their jobs. Mr Reg Campbell, in charge of the cellars and bar supplies, a knowledgeable man jealously proud of his department and it immaculate condition, was faced with the knotty problem of dealing with the thousand of empty bottles from the bar. During the season as many as 3,700 dozen had to be disposed of in a week, and he had to work out a system for dealing with them neatly, quickly and with minimum breakages.

He tried a number of methods involving hosepipes from the bars to the cellars; the bottles were dropped down these pipes, landing on a large table, the size of a billiard table in the cellar. The idea was that they would be collected and sorted before crating, but their speed down the hosepipe broke far too many making it impossible to collect and sort them The solution was found in narrower hosepipes fitted with rubber flaps at the end to break the fall of the bottles. These were shot neatly into

A celebration in the backyard of a Kirkham public house a few days after the completion of the Tower in 1894. Walter Smith, the third man from the left in the back row, had worked on the building of the Tower as a ganger.

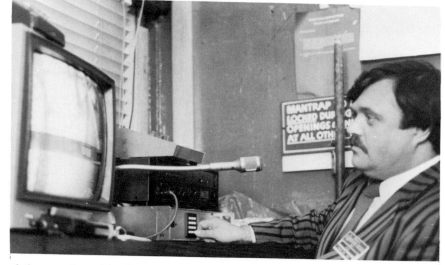

Right: A member of the Tower staff keeps an eye on the closed-circuit television which monitors activities at the Tower top.

Below right: A warning to visitors who might be wondering how long it will take an object to reach the ground from the Tower top.

an open-ended box and then to the table, from which they could be taken and sorted. This solution resulted in fewer than ten dozen breakages a week, a figure which the management considered quite acceptable.

The dedication of the staff applies just as much today as it did in the Bickerstaffe era. One octogenarian who retired many years ago cannot stay away from the Tower, and during the season is usually to be found helping out in a change dispenser. Although the servility and subservience of pre-war days has gone, one cannot but be impressed today with the friendliness and helpfulness of the staff at all levels. They are intensely proud of *their* Tower, and how a surprising knowledge of the structure and its history, which they are always ready to explain carefully to an interested visitor.

The liftmen are still subject to endless unoriginal jokes from the passengers, and bear them with smiling fortitude: "Your life is full of ups and downs, isn't it?", or "You do have an uplifting job". And "I suppose you've got to the top of your profession" when the lift arrives. Sometimes the liftmen get their own back. One liftman could not resist asking, when a priest entered the lift, "Are you going up to head office, Father?"

At the Tower top attendants keep a watchful eye on all three levels with ten closed-circuit TV cameras which give a view of all four sides of the platforms. Foolhardy attempts at stunts and displays of bravado are firmly discouraged; one man did succeed in jumping from the first platform and was killed when he crashed through a ventilator on the level below.

A bearded man who threatened to jump during his forty-one-hour sit-in at the Tower top was coerced down peacefully after being given an assurance that no action would be taken against him. Given the title of "Bird Man of the Tower" by the press, this man sought to stage a protest against what he regarded as excessive police powers.

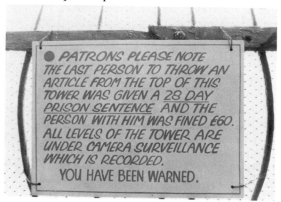

● PATRONS PLEASE NOTE THE LAST PERSON TO THROW AN ARTICLE FROM THE TOP OF THIS TOWER WAS GIVEN A 28 DAY PRISON SENTENCE AND THE PERSON WITH HIM WAS FINED £60. ALL LEVELS OF THE TOWER ARE UNDER CAMERA SURVEILLANCE WHICH IS RECORDED. YOU HAVE BEEN WARNED.

The postmark introduced for postcards posted from the Tower top.

After the 1897 fire a gift shop was opened at the Tower top from which visitors could buy souvenirs and picture postcards. During the nineteen-fifties Mr William McGinty, then house manager, introduced a postal arrangement whereby picture postcards could be posted at the top of the Tower and had the postmark "Blackpool Tower" impressed on them, thus proving that the sender had made this historic ascent; that is still a feature today.

Apart from the usual collection of inscribed souvenirs, today's holidaymakers can also purchase impressive certificates declaring that they have made the ascent, which they can proudly frame and display on their walls. Those who wish can also purchase certificates saying they were too cowardly to make the journey.

With no sinister intent but with merely a desire for publicity, some Manchester University students celebrated rag day in 1962 by climbing the icy Tower at night and planting a huge flag in the crow's nest 500 feet above the promenade. The students, between the ages of nineteen and twenty-one, were spotted by a security guard, to whom they explained that they were experienced mountaineers.

Authorised stunts are occasionally permitted by the management, and stringent precautions to ensure the safety of those taking part are always carried out. In the nineteen-eighties a jet-propelled space-suited man scorned the use of the lifts and simply jetted up to the platform, watched by a large crowd on the promenade. Another event that attracted a crowd was the wedding of escapologist Karl Bartoni, who was married at the Tower top. In 1984 an eighty-four-foot high King Kong was suspended from the side of the Tower; a giant inflated figure with a menacing snarl on his face, he caused more amusement than fear when he developed a puncture and began to sag in a very undignified manner.

While all these stunts offer both the Tower and Blackpool invaluable publicity, they do present the Tower Company with a lot of headaches. Although charitable stunts may receive consideration, commercial ventures are usually discouraged. All the same, on one occasion a car sales firm persuaded Douglas Bickerstaffe to allow them to give a demonstration of the strength of a new car's springs and suspension at the entrance to North Pier by borrowing a circus elephant which would stand on the car. The demonstration was much publicised, and a large crowd gathered to watch as the large, amiable elephant sauntered along the Promenade to the car, examined it disdainfully with its trunk, and, at the urging of its handler, obligingly stepped on to it. Immediately, with a loud cracking, the springs and suspension collapsed and the tyres burst, and the elephant bowed in gratification at the delighted applause of the onlookers.

For years Blackpool Tower was the established holiday favourite with Lancashire and

Above: *Looking east from the top of the Tower, with the Winter Gardens in the foreground.*

BL CKPOOL
TOWER

**518'9"
Tower Top
Lift Ride**

*This is to Certify that
on ____
____ was too cowardly
to venture 518'9" to
the top of Blackpool
Tower. St Bootsasters*

(Lift Control Officer)

Official Seal

Right: *Among the souvenirs available at the Tower is this certificate for those who do not make the ascent.*

Left: *The man who "flew" to the top of the Tower using a jet-pack.*

Opposite page, below: *Three Tower pensioners, Reginald Dixon, Charlie Cairoli and Charles Barlow, on Blackpool beach.*

Below: *An advertisement for the Tower adorns this Blackpool tram. Blackpool is the last town in Britain to have an electric tramway system; it celebrated its centenary in 1985.*

Yorkshire visitors, but its fame was extended nationally and internationally by regular broadcasts from the Tower by various bands and by the Wurlitzer organist, usually Reginald Dixon. In 1950 "Woman's Hour" was devoted entirely to the Tower; Kathleen Williams appeared for the management, Annette of the Children's Ballet was interviewed, and there were tunes from Reginald Dixon and a visit to the circus quarters in Staining.

When television arrived with the opening of Holme Moss transmitter in 1951 signals were relayed from London to the top of the Tower and then to Holme Moss, and the country saw Blackpool Tower on television for the first time. If John Bickerstaffe thought that the showing of the first movie film in the ballroom nearly half a century earlier had been history in the making, surely he would have regarded this as another historical milestone.

A charismatic trio stands out supreme in Tower history: Charlie Cairoli, Charles Barlow and Reginald Dixon, each of whom served the Tower and its patrons for forty years or more. If the Tower made them famous, they in turn made the Tower famous.

The lifeblood pulsing through the Tower's veins is the customers. When Sir John said in 1894 that the Tower needed at least 750,000 visitors a year to be a paying proposition, he thought he was being over-optimistic; he was delighted when his target was almost immediately reached. How much it would have pleased him to know that ninety years later no fewer than 1.3 million visitors a year were passing through the Tower. The Eiffel Tower proudly announced that by 1983 they had reached their hundred millionth visitor, but that figure had long ago been exceeded by the Blackpool Tower.

Yesterday and Tomorrow 16

WHY WAS IT that, of so many proposed towers, only two in Britain reached completion? And why, of those two, has Blackpool Tower alone survived?

Historians might well speculate on the reasons for failure or success. Shortage of cash was undoubtedly one of the main causes of failure; there is no doubt that the Blackpool Tower Company suffered from an acute shortage of cash in its early days, yet it survived. And the Blackpool company was faced by much local antagonism, something which does not seem to have been aroused by proposals for towers elsewhere.

What was there that Blackpool Tower had that all the others lacked? One is forced to the conclusion that the single positive factor contributing to its success and to its survival was the strength of purpose of the indomitable John Bickerstaffe, without which the Tower would surely have died in its infancy.

For John, the three years from the formation of the Blackpool Tower Company in 1891 to the opening of the Tower to the public in 1894 were worrying ones. When the visitors queued up in their thousands to travel in the lifts to see what no man had ever seen before, the Lancashire coastline from the air, he felt that his faith in the project had after all been justified.

After having suffered so many early setbacks and so many objections to his plans, he must have been pleased to find himself accepted by his fellow townsmen. When the local council in 1912 presented him with the Freedom of the Borough of Blackpool John regarded this as a tribute to the Tower and a recognition of what it had done for the town. The contribution he had made not just to Blackpool's prosperity but to the prestige of Britain was recognized in 1926 with the award of a knighthood. The Tower Company directors paid their own tribute to him by designating one of the rooms Sir John's Room.

Sir John never forgot his fishing background, however. He could be seen on every occasion wearing a white-covered sailor's peaked cap, though in every other respect he appeared to be the typical Edwardian businessman.

On Sir John's death his only son Robert was elected to the board as a director, and his younger brother Tom, always known locally as Alderman Tom, became chairman of the company. When Tom died four years later Robert became chairman, remaining in the chair right through the Second World War. On his retirement in 1945 his cousin Douglas, Alderman Tom's son, was elected chairman.

Like his father in appearance, Douglas was well built with a ruddy countenance, a keen sense of humour, and his father's blunt speech; he also had his uncle's dedication and love of the Tower. He was educated at a private school in Blackpool and went on to university at Heidelberg in Germany, being interned during the First World War. When he left university after the war he worked for a time with the American Express Company until returning to Blackpool to run his father's fleet of paddle steamers from the North Pier. One of the boats

was the old *Bickerstaffe*; the choice of name prompted his friend Harold Grime, grandson of John Grime, who had opposed so vigorously the original Tower proposal, to write in the *Blackpool Gazette*, "This is the first time a Bickerstaffe was all at sea". The *Bickerstaffe* was scrapped in 1928.

Douglas was something of a philanthropist. In 1938 he told the chairman of the Blackpool Children's Pantomime to book a hundred seats for the show for poor girls and boys in Blackpool and to send the bill to him. He repeated this request the following year, increasing the number to five hundred children and giving each child a Christmas present as well.

Despite his education, he never lost his Lancashire accent; indeed, on occasions he tended to emphasize it. When the Queen and the Duke of Edinburgh attended a Royal Variety Performance in the Opera House of the Winter Gardens in 1955, the Queen looked around her admiringly and remarked to Douglas what a handsome building it was. Nodding offhandedly, Douglas said in broad Lancashire tones, "Ay, I suppose so, although it's nobbut an annexe to't'Tower!"

Rarely a day passed without Douglas making an appearance in the Tower, smoking Woodbine cigarettes, with the ash dropping down his waistcoat, watching the dancers in the ballroom, standing at the back of the circus, or just wandering about the place, saying little but noticing everything. His comments would later be passed to the appropriate head of department; but the staff knew he could always be approached with problems or questions about the running of day-to-day affairs.

Douglas was, sadly, the last of the Bickerstaffes on the board. Shortly after his retirement in 1963 the directors agreed to accept an offer for their company. For a decade, through changes of ownership and management, the Tower appeared to drift on a sea of indifference. Little investment was ploughed back, and the regular programme of improvement, restoration and maintenance so assiduously followed by each of the Bickerstaffes was woefully neglected.

In 1980 Charles Forte, who had previously acquired the North and South Piers, bought the Tower Company and all its property from EMI for £16 million, but it did not fit comfortably into the Forte organization. With the possibility of the company's property being split up and sold off to individual buyers—an unthinkable prospect—Lord Delfont formed a company called First Leisure which purchased the whole concern for £43 million in 1982. The complex acquired by First Leisure comprised the Tower, the Winter Gardens, both with their shops and buildings, three piers, and considerable property not only in and around Blackpool but also in other parts of the country.

Above right: *Lord Delfont, who formed a company to acquire the whole of the Tower concern in 1982.*

Right: *The new lounge, as rebuilt after the 1956 fire.*

Today the Tower has regained its former strength and vigour. Considerable amounts of cash have been ploughed back in the essential up-dating, alteration and restoration; in 1984 alone practically the whole interior was decorated or altered, over £2 million being reinvested.

The large combines have not been the only buyers of the Tower. She has probably been sold as often as the Blackpool trams, for which there is a regular seasonal trade by the tricksters to the gullible. One man who eagerly bought what the plausible salesman assured him was the lift "concession" (when there was a separate charge for the ascent) sat all day by the lift kiosk totting up his takings, which at the end of the day he demanded; he became understandably annoyed when told that he had been conned.

Traditionalists might regret, and even deplore, some of the changes at the Tower, but if the Tower is to maintain its popularity it has to move with the times. In the past forty years there have been great changes in the kind of leisure activities demanded by holidaymakers, and these changes in demand have dictated the policies followed by the Tower management. Even those who bemoan the loss of the Roof Gardens must admit that the replacement, "Jungle Jim's", provides a far greater attraction—to the children, at least.

Whatever modernization has been carried

The painted ceiling and lavish decoration of the ballroom has remained unchanged through the years.

Changing styles of children's
entertainment in the Tower.
Above is a corner of "Jungle
Jim's", which allows the
youngsters to work off their
energy, and on the **right** is a
Punch and Judy show in the
Roof Gardens in an earlier
period.

Left: *One of the Tower's guardians, a stone figure on the outside of the building.* Royal Commission on Historical Monuments (England)

Right: *The Ocean Room, showing the modern decor.*

Below: *The gilded decoration of one of the loudspeaker grilles in the ballroom.*

out, a favourite part of the Tower premises has not been altered at all. The magnificent ballroom remains very much as it has been from the beginning, and it is still the place where romances begin and blossom; what does it matter that some of today's dancers are informally dressed—for one wonderful evening they can escape from reality into a world of colour, glamour and glitter, with their loved ones clasped in their arms.

As the Tower approaches its centenary it still throbs with life. Hundreds of thousands of visitors surge through the doors each year, trampling over the specially designed carpets and subjecting them to just as much wear in a week as those of the average large hotel receive in a lifetime. Most of the visitors seem oblivious of the treasures so proudly displayed from the Tower's past and quite unaware of the historical background of Lancashire's most noted landmark. They know only that each year the Tower looks as fresh as paint and

comes up with new ideas and new attractions to ensure that they have a thoroughly enjoyable holiday; it is the perfect leisure trendsetter.

With its perennially fascinating view from the top, the Tower itself is a monument to a unique form of Victorian architecture; the buildings at its base form a curious time-capsule of one hundred years of entertainment, incorporating the traditions of the Victorian era, the adventures of today, and the promise of tomorrow's space age. The displays of classical art and decor rarely found in a place of amusement today cannot fail to astonish and delight present-day historians and art students as much as they did their pleasure-seeking ancestors in the last century.

Sir John's claim that the Tower was "The Wonderland of the World" is as appropriate today as it ever was. As Mr Keith West, the present manager of the Tower and as devoted to his charge as any Bickerstaffe, so aptly puts it: "The Tower is leisure in a looking glass".

THE BLACKPOOL TOWER.

MESSRS. MAXWELL AND TUKE, ARCHITECTS, MANCHESTER.

(For Description, see Page **343**.)

Fig.1.

Left: *A technical drawing of the Tower as originally built.*

Below: *Plans showing the foundations for one of the legs.*

APPENDIX ONE

The Tower Structure*

THE TOWER is a steel structure, 500 feet high and weighing approximately 2,500 tons. The foundations are in boulder clay and consist of four large blocks of concrete 35 feet square and 12 feet thick under the four legs of the Tower. Steel grillages were embedded into the concrete to distribute the pressure of the leg pillars evenly over it.

On top of the joists are four steel bedplates, and on these rest the base girders of the legs. The base girders are of box section, 3 feet deep by 2 feet 4 inches wide, and are joined together so as to form a frame 16 feet 6 inches square, at the corners, on which rest the four main pillars of the leg. The base girders are each held down by four steel bolts 3¼ inches diameter at each corner, making sixteen to each leg and sixty-four in all, which pass through base girders and concrete, and are secured to cast-iron washer plates at the bottom.

The base girders are also extended to the outside of the Tower to the main keep walls, which affords additional weight for resisting any tendency to lift on the windward side.

The first main floor is at the 55-feet level, which is also the starting point of the main ascent hoists. The next main floor is at the 85-feet level, which also forms part of the main roof of the building. From then to the 380-feet level the structure is of lattice construction at each horizontal or bracing level connecting to

the four legs, which are of box construction, the pillars being 2 feet 3 inches square at the base, tapering to 12 inches square at the upper floor levels.

The tie rods between each floor level, bracing the structure diagonally against sheer-

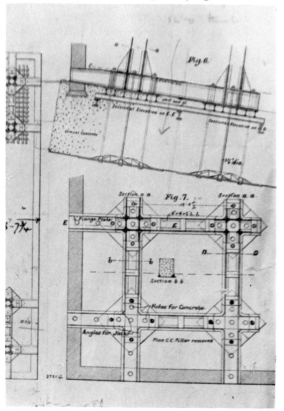

*From a report compiled in 1958 by Mr G. Foster, chief engineer to Blackpool Tower Company, 1952–62.

121

ing stress, vary from 3¼ inches diameter to 2 inches diameter.

From the 380-feet level at which the lift ascent terminates up to the 430-feet level various concrete platforms are formed, accessible to the public by staircases to form promenades. The four legs terminate just above this level, the rest of the structure being of light construction, mostly angle bar and flat bar fabrication. The flag pole is of tubular steel and is 60 feet long and weighs 30 cwt, 35 feet of its length being enclosed inside the structure itself.

The Tower structure has been practically rebuilt from the 85-feet level upwards since 1920, approximately forty men being employed twelve months of the year in cutting out and replacing defective parts and in the continuous repainting.

All steel is fabricated in the company's premises, each defective piece being used as a template for the new one. Mild steel angles and plates up to 35 feet long and 4 inches × 4 inches × ½ inch section and 15 inches ×

½-inch section gives some idea what renewals mean in terms of length and size.

The entire construction is riveted, but of late years electric arc welding has been used with success to combat corrosion, and where possible for fabrication. But being a riveted structure this has to be kept within well defined limits, otherwise strain and stress would arise, which do not apply to a riveted structure, with disastrous results.

Before work can be commenced on any part of the structure elaborate precautions have to be taken to ensure safety to surrounding property with outrigged safety netting, scaffolding for working platforms and sheeting for wind breakage for the workmen. At the upper levels, wind speeds of 75 mph are not uncommon, and up-currents, caused by the configuration of the structure, of 90 mph have been measured.

The deflection from the vertical at the 380-feet level in a 70 mph gale has been measured as being only 1 inch from the vertical.

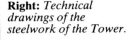

Right: *Technical drawings of the steelwork of the Tower.*

Left: *Two "stick-men" at work on the structure during winter maintenance.*

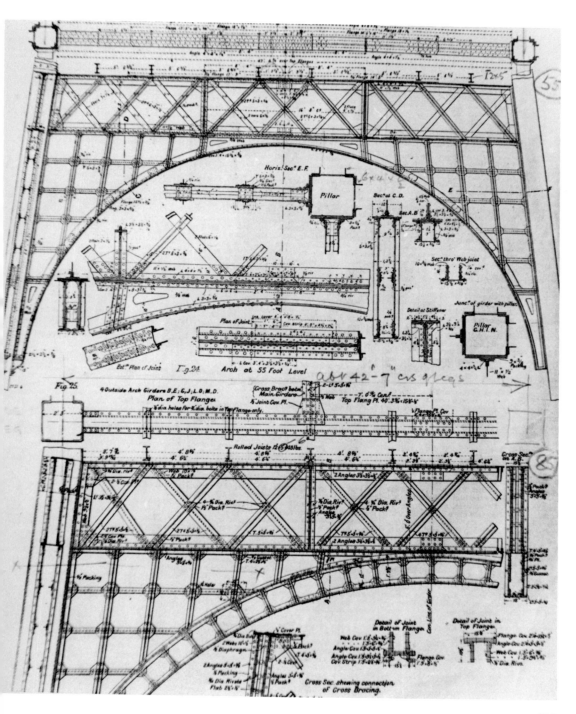

Fig. 24.   Arch at 55 Foot Level

Fig. 25.   4 Outside Arch Girders B, E, G, J, L, O, M, D.
Plan of Top Flanges

Cross Sec. shewing connection of Cross Bracing.

Detail of Joint in Bottom Flange.

Detail of Joint in Top Flange.

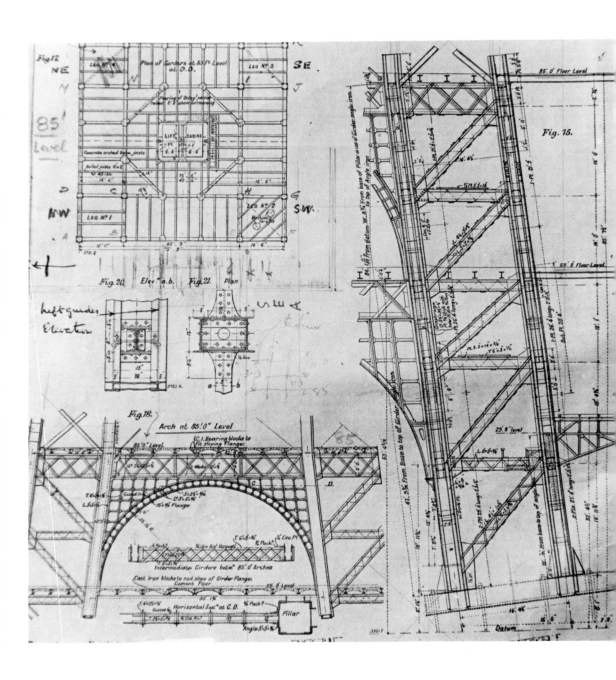

*Drawings showing the construction of the legs
and platforms.*

124

APPENDIX TWO

The Tower Ascent

THE ASCENT of the Blackpool Tower is made by two independent lifts. The cars are hauled by four $13/16$-inch steel cables, with a breaking strain of 20 tons each, and also from the car to the counterweight by five $5/8$-inch steel cables with a breaking strain of 12.5 ton. The flying counterweight is suspended by a 2:1 rope reduction; its weight is 11 tons.

The car weight is 6 ton, and this shows the car to be ½ ton out of balance to the counterweight so that the car can always be returned to the ground if there is a failure of the power supply.

The lifts were originally hydraulically operated, but after sixty years' service it was decided to renew the equipment with an electrically operated system. The conversion commenced in 1952 and was completed in 1957, and during this period no running time was lost. The main contractors for this scheme were Otis Elevator Co. Ltd and the sub-contractors Robey's of Lincoln; Otis were responsible for the electrical equipment, generators, control panels, etc., and Robey's for the main winding drums and the brake system.

Owing to the size of the equipment it was necessary to build a complete new lifthouse on the roof of the building, although this position was not accessible from the street. This meant that every piece of equipment had to be broken down and carried up through the building into position.

The whole of the equipment sits on three plate girders fastened between the inner legs on the west side of the Tower; they are approximately 39 feet long. These were taken on to the side and spliced together in the lifthouse. The weight of each winder drum with brake equipment, etc., is approximately 20 tons per lift. The winder drums are 8 feet in diameter and the driving motor is a DC shunt wound machine of 120 hp.

The original car was left in service and given slightly improved appearance. The car speed is rated at 200 feet per minute. There is a rope safety device attached to the car suspension so that should any one of the four main hauling ropes become slack or be out of tension with the lift car the brake shoes are applied to the main structure and it is held firm.

Other safety devices are fitted in the lifthouse:

If a power failure takes place while the lift is in motion a brake is de-energised and this applies the main winder brakes.
Overspeed in any direction is covered by a governor, and if it exceeds the normal speed by 20% the brake is applied.
If the car should be jammed in the shaft while travelling in the "up" direction, one of several overload devices will trip the control circuit. If travelling in the "down" direction a slack rope device operates and trips the control circuit.
Manually operated foot release.

There are four brake shoes fitted to each winder drum, and they are so designed that any one pair will hold a fully loaded car. Again, should a lift be made inoperative in any part of the shaft, it can be returned to ground level by a hand operated brake release in the lifthouse, due to its being out of balance with the counterweight.

The total distance travelled by the lift car for the public is from the 65-foot level in the building to the 380-foot level, at the Tower top. The stopping of the lift at the top and bottom levels is controlled by the lift driver, but if for any reason he cannot operate his control handle, the lift is stopped automatically by shaft limits and control limits in the lifthouse.

Before the lifts were electrified they were hydraulically operated, water being the pumping fluid used. The gas engines and triple ram pumps installed in 1894 were later replaced by two 175 hp three-phase slip ring motors driving two 10-stage centrifugal mining pumps, delivering pressure at 475 lb per square inch at 1,500 rpm.

This pressure was led to three storage accumulators situated in the base of the southwest leg. The pistons of these accumulators were 2 feet 3 inches in diameter and their stroke or travel 17 feet 0 inches in the vertical. Each piston was dead-weighted with cast iron blocks to 120 tons to give the required pressure on the system. Six-inch bore pipelines took the pressure to the hydraulic pistons situated in the same leg between the 85-foot level and the 35-foot level.

As the travel of the lifts is 325 feet we obviously cannot have a ram or piston of the same length to move the same distance, so we resort to the simple method of a block and tackle to solve the problem. With a two to one reduction on a tackle gear, for every foot travelled on the hauling rope 6 inches are travelled on the hoisting sheave. Also for every pound weight exerted 2 pounds are lifted. Therefore, with a 10 to 1 reduction, for every foot travelled on the hoisting sheave, 10 feet are travelled on the hauling rope. No allowance is made here for frictional losses, etc.

The hydraulic pistons were 21 inches in diameter, giving a pull of 73 tons, with twin piston rods 3¼ inches diameter and a stroke of 32 feet 6 inches, the ends of the rods being

The hoist room, with the winding drums visible towards the left.

126

Part of the hydraulic lift machinery which was used until the nineteen-fifties.

anchored to the bottom section of the reduction gearing. Four main hoisting ropes 13/16 inches in diameter led through these sheaves to suspend the lift, with a total breaking strain of 88 tons. To reduce the lifting force required, the lift cages were also counterweighted through a two to one reduction sheaving to counterweights weighing approximately 11 tons each, which travel up and down the north-east leg of the structure. There are five ropes 5/8 inches in diameter to each counterweight with a total breaking strain of 70 tons. The combined ropes give a safety factor of about 20 to 1.

In each lift cabin was a handwheel driving a worm and reduction gearing which operated what was termed the handrope, whose function was to open and close the main throttle valve in the pistons to allow pressure to be admitted and exhausted to the pistons, whichever the case might be, for lifting or lowering. Assuming the lift to be at the bottom, the pistons would be at the full extent of their travel, the

reduction sheaving in a closed position and the balance weight at its highest level. On operating the handwheel in the lift cabin, the main throttle valve on the pistons was opened and pressure was applied from the storage accumulators. The pistons now moved downwards, the weight applied was consequently greater than the lift cabin, and for every foot the reduction sheaving opened ten feet was travelled by the lift. At the end of the run the throttle valve was closed. With the cylinder full of water and locked in by the valves, the lift remained at rest.

To bring the lift down the throttle valve was opened to exhaust. The pressure being released from the cylinder, the weight of the lift overcame the weight of the balance weight, piston rods, sheaving, etc.

Remember the block and tackle, how easy it is on the hauling end of the rope? It will be seen that by admitting varying volumes of water at pressure, or by exhausting varying volumes, by means of the throttle valve, so the speed of the lift could be varied at will or the lift could be brought to rest in any desired position.

Automatic choke-valves were installed in conjunction with the main throttle valves which brought the lift to floor levels at the top and bottom of the run without the assistance of the operator.

The lift cabins weigh approximately 6 tons each, and will hold 25 persons to each cabin. The time taken for the ascent by hydraulic power was 55 seconds, equal to a speed of 350 feet per minute. The speed of descent was a lot faster, 33 seconds, 600 feet per minute travel.

On a busy day the lifts have been known to make 500 complete trips in 14 hours of continuous running, carrying 12,000 persons to the top of the ascent and down again. The upper platforms of the structure are capable of accommodating 600 persons at one time. It is interesting to note that in one day the lifts travel a distance of 60 miles, which compares, say, with the distance from Blackpool to Chester.

One pump was sufficient to supply power for both lifts, and the electrical controls of the slip ring motors could be hand operated or entirely automatic as desired, according to the number of trips run and the pressure drawn from the accumulators. The accumulators stored enough energy for one lift to make three complete trips of the ascent if the pumping gear should fail.

As frequently happens with intermittent running, the accumulators became fully charged, the pumps then delivering against a full head of water. They were so designed that on a 3% rise above normal working pressure, the delivery of the pumps dropped to about a third of its value. Thus the delivery from the pump ceased and circulation was within the pump housing itself, until the volume of water contained in the accumulators was reduced again by the working of the lift pistons.

The pumps were fitted with Mitchell thrust bearings to eliminate end play, and to provide an equal balance of all moving parts.

Advantage was taken of the hydraulic power to run a large water spectacle in the Tower Circus, and also several small goods lifts which operated from basement to ground floor level.

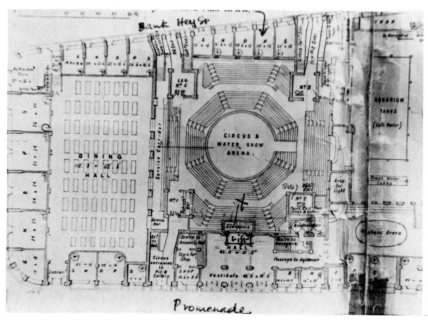

Drawings showing the Tower Circus and, on the right, part of the Aquarium.

APPENDIX THREE

The Circus

THE CIRCUS arena is situated inside the four legs of the Tower, the actual floor area is 42 feet in diameter, and the capacity is 2,500 persons.

The ring can be turned into a huge water tank for staging elaborate water spectacles, and hydraulic power for this is derived from the same source as that employed for the main ascent lifts when they were operated by hydraulic pressure. Picture the arena walls as an open-ended cylinder and the arena floor as a large piston and piston rod working inside the cylinder, the cylinder being a brick-lined tank 42 feet in diameter and 7 feet deep, and filled with water to a depth of 6 feet. Inside this is the arena floor or piston, 4 feet 9 inches in diameter and about 1 foot deep, supported on a centre piston rod or hydraulic ram, with a cylinder buried in the foundations of the arena. The piston is 18½ inches diameter and capable of displacing about 40 tons deadweight.

In the normal working position the piston is at the top of its stroke and resting on chocks, with the water in the tank below. To flood the ring the piston is moved round on its centre by a hydraulic ram to displace it off its chocks, then pressure is exhausted from the main cylinder. The deadweight of the floor and piston then forces the piston into the tank, the water escaping to the top of the piston through slots provided in the floor and through the gap all round between the circumference of the floor and the cylinder walls. To raise the floor, pressure is applied to the cylinder and the ram forces the floor up through the water. Approximately 42,000 gallons of water are displaced in 60 seconds, and the weight of the floor and piston is estimated at 14 tons.

Water for the swimming tank is taken direct from the freshwater mains and then passed through modern sand filtering equipment. When swimming acts are required the water is also heated by steam calorifiers to about 70 degrees F. Filtration is carried out daily to remove all matter that may be left on the arena floor, and the water is also chemically treated to give it the clarity and sparkle necessary for swimming baths by chlorination, alumina and aeration.

Inside the Circus.

APPENDIX FOUR

The Tower Aquarium

THE ORIGINAL Aquarium was opened in 1874, and during the building of the Tower structure with its Circus, Ballroom, etc., the Aquarium structure was incorporated as one of the attractions.

In 1936 extensive widening on the north side and alterations and renewals were carried out. New fish tanks, pumps, filtering equipment and refrigerating gear were installed, replacing the old sand and gravel filters and ammonia refrigerating gear to make the Aquarium the interesting feature it is today.

Water circulation

From the main collecting tanks in the basement the centrifugal pumps take the water and deliver up to what are called the gravity tanks, which are placed above the fish tanks. From here it is piped by gravity flow to the fish tanks. The rate of flow is controlled by valves, and constant charge and level are maintained by overflow pipes placed in each tank. All overflows are collected and returned to the collecting tanks, and the surplus water is delivered to the gravity tanks. The circulation pumps are 4 inch suction, 3 inch deliveries giving 100 gallons per minute at 60 foot head, at a speed of 1450 rpm.

Filtration

As the pumps deliver the water to the gravity tanks it is first by-passed to a battery of filters, forcing the water through the sand prior to delivery to the tanks. The filters contain about

three tons of coarse sand each, and are equipped with motor-driven agitating arms for stirring the sand when washing out, by means of a battery of freshwater sprays connected to a separate main. Both the pumps and the filters run day and night, and there are duplicate equipments, as a breakdown would mean a loss of all the fish in a very short time due to lack of fresh air.

Refrigeration

Both the salt and freshwater main collecting tanks are fitted with cooling systems. Two 10 hp twin-cylinder water-cooled compressor units are installed. The expansion coils are totally submerged in the salt and freshwater tanks, and are formed of large banks of one-inch solid drawn heavy gauge copper tubing. The compressors are fitted with both hand and automatic controls, and thermostats immersed in the tanks ensure a fine limit of control, maintaining the water at 56 degrees F. Freon gas was chosen as the refrigerant because it is classified as non-poisonous, and it was thought that no ill-effects would be caused to the fish should a leak occur in the coils; as the gas is non-soluble in water it escapes to free air as bubbles before it can be pumped into the fish tanks proper.

Tropical fish

These species are maintained in a special section of tanks kept at 75 degrees F, which is the average temperature of tropical waters.

130

There is a small fish hatchery on the roof of the buildings for breeding tropicals.

Replacements

Replacements of fish for the main tanks are kept up by the company's own staff by rod and line fishing from ponds, rivers and jetties, and also from deep sea trawling expeditions. For these expeditions specially designed tanks having an air supply maintained by compressed air cylinders are carried on the ships, and they can be lifted by crane direct from the ship's deck on to lorries for transport to the Aquarium. Many fish arrive by air, also in specially designed tanks and containers.

Acknowledgements to Mr G. Foster; *Engineering*, 3rd May, 1895; Babcock Robey's of Lincoln.

BLACKPOOL TOWER MEASUREMENTS:

Aquarium: 146 × 62 feet
Menagerie: 112 × 69 feet
Elevator Hall: 110 × 110 feet
Circus: 110 × 110 feet
Ballroom: 120 × 102 feet

COMPARABLE TOWER WEIGHTS AND COSTS:

	Eiffel:	Blackpool:	New Brighton:
Opening date:	1889	1894	1898
Cost:	£298,000	£45,000	£60,000
Weight:	7,000 tons	2,600 tons	1,760 tons
Height:	984 feet	500 feet	576 feet

(All heights are quoted without flagpoles or aerials.)

Index

Illustrations in bold type